*Esna,*

# How to Land Your
# First Million-Dollar Listing

*Wishing you a Million-Dollar Year!*

*Jane Bond*

*2021*

# J A N E   B O N D

PAGE PUBLISHING, INC.
Conneaut Lake, PA

First originally published by Page Publishing 2020

ISBN 978-1-6624-0290-6 (pbk)
ISBN 978-1-6624-0291-3 (digital)

Printed in the United States of America

# TESTIMONIALS

....................................

"I absolutely loved your book. As an editor and a published author myself, I can honestly say you've written something great. You're a great storyteller. Your book isn't just informational. I was pleasantly surprised that you included dialogue that kept me engaged, amused, and inspired. You had some very funny dialogue and inner thoughts throughout the book. You are not just teaching real estate agents the business, but your book has an inspirational component to it. If I was a real estate agent, this book would definitely inspire and encourage me to keep going and be the best at what I do. Because of this, I can honesty give this book a 10!"

—Rothesia Stokes, published author

"In thinking about the world of real estate, for me, I attach one name with the adjectives *professional, honest,* and *pulls no punches* the name that comes to mind is that of Jane Bond!

Her work ethic is undeniable or, as I would call it, top drawer! We all know that when you refer any professional, the end result of that relationship always reflects on the person who makes the referral.

When I refer Jane Bond I actually sleep like a baby and never concern myself with one of my clients being unhappy! A role model and a person we could all learn from."

—Steven Gurowitz, president

*Interiors*
*Interior Design* *by Steven G. Inc.*

"As friends of Jane for over two decades, and some of her first clients, Dawn and I have always been impressed with her exquisite creativity and poise. She has helped us to beautify and design incredible spaces for our large family. Her knowledge and expertise is second to none. The only thing Jane does not know how to do is to operate in a manner that is less than excellent! She embodies integrity and the utmost professionalism at all times. What we admire most about her, though, is her sincere heart full of loyalty and her deep desire to give her clients the most amazing experience from idea to execution. We are privileged to count her as a professional we can trust, but we are most honored that she considers us as friends."

—Harry Swayne, MA, SCP, three-time Super Bowl Champion Dawn Swayne, Certified Life Coach

"Jane is one of the hardest-working women I know. Her drive and commitment to operate in excellence is truly unmatched. One thing I love about Jane is no matter the task, she always manages to figure it out and get things done. Her advice is always real and spot on. There is no challenge that she can't face in life no matter how big or small. Her spirit is genuine, and she's all about the only thing that matters at the end of the day—happiness. If you aren't happy in whatever you're pursuing, Jane is the first one to tell you to do something else. She sees the good and the potential in everyone. She is passionate about helping others. Our relationship started out as business but has evolved into so much more! I look up to Jane like a sister, and I'm sure I wouldn't have the confidence I have today had she not come into my life. Jane is the definition of success. Throughout her life, she's faced many challenges but still managed to come out on top in each of her career paths. My friend and my sister—a true wealth of knowledge and wisdom is who and what she is."

—Rashauna Scott, agent investor, founder of Flippin in Heels

"When I think of Jane Bond, the words *phenomenal, superior, best in class*, and *authentic* immediately come to mind. I met Jane in 2014 when my family and I were moving from Atlanta to Naples, Florida, and because of Jane, we were able to find and purchase a beautiful place to call our home. Today as I reflect on our path, I realize how much of a blessing it was to have THE best of the best as my agent and even better, a great and true friend. Jane exudes a winning attitude every time. Her service and delivery are top-notch. Best of all—she listens, understands, and proves that she truly cares about her clients. Thank you, Jane, for sharing your inspirational story and for being our beacon of light through our journey."

—Tricia Walcott, senior vice president (SVP), Top 10 Fortune 500 Bank

I dedicate this book to my best friend John Jones, who always stood by my side as my biggest cheerleader and encouraged me to do whatever I thought, I wanted to do because he believed I could. I was his Superwoman and Bondgirl.

Our light will shine forever together. Unfortunately, my best friend John Jones passed away on March 12, 2019 RIP

# CONTENTS

Introduction ......................................................................11

1.  Who's Your Partner? ...............................................15
2.  My Big Why ..........................................................25
3.  When the Lights Came On ........................................32
4.  Your Customer or Your Money....................................41
5.  The Realization .....................................................49
6.  The Breakdown Before the Breakthrough.....................57
7.  Networking Is Key ..................................................66
8.  It's Showtime.........................................................77
9.  The Marketing Game...............................................82
10. Playing in the Sandbox............................................90
11. Selling a Rock Star.................................................99
12. Who's the Real Baller? ...........................................105

Acknowledgments ...............................................................117

# INTRODUCTION

Looking back on growing up as a kid in Philadelphia, I can remember how I used to sit on my stoop and dream about the life I wanted to have in the future. I always knew what nice things were and what quality looked like, but being able to attain this life and the things I desired was another story in my life at that time.

My mother was a registered nurse who worked the night shift, and my father was a bar and nightclub owner. The great thing was that my mom was always there each morning to make us breakfast and get us ready for school. However, the mind shift did not click until my dad retired my mom from her day job as a nurse and made her an entrepreneur and bar owner. My mom was already a hard worker and wanted nothing but the best for us.

Therefore, working until the wee hours of the morning in her own business did not faze her at all. I saw how our lives slowly started to change while watching my mom turn into a happier mom.

Even though she was working longer hours, she seemed to be working smarter in her own business and making more money to contribute to the family pot.

I started to notice that we could afford nicer furniture, clothes, and cars as we got older, and going to college was an option. This was a mind-set shift for me. Watching them grow exponentially on their own terms was something I knew I wanted to do as well.

They did not work nine to five. They seemed to work all the time, but they created their own schedule, made more money, and was able to give us a better lifestyle.

What my parents actually did was lay a foundation that taught me, if I worked for myself and worked with the same work ethic and determination, I could provide a great lifestyle for myself and my future family.

We definitely had our share of bar troubles with fights, drugs, theft, and burglary.

However, at the time, it seemed normal, and we just kept our wits about us at all times when we were at the bars. If you can imagine late seventies, early eighties.

My dad would take me and my youngest sister, Stephanie, everywhere with him. I guess he called himself teaching us the business too. He taught us how to do inventory on the first-in, first-out (FIFO) system, count money quickly, and fire people when we caught them stealing because we were a cash business.

Of course, I handled the books for inventory, so I knew exactly how many shots were in a bottle, glasses of wine in a gallon, and beers in a case. So most of the time, I turned out to be the bad girl.

My first attempt at entrepreneurship was at one of Dad's bars called Dauphin Street West. Now our bars were not in the suburbs; they were in the hood. In retrospect, I would even say the area was much more rough than I would like to remember.

I opened up a little kitchen over top of the bar and called it Karen's Kitchen. This is a really funny story. When I was about fifteen, I was at a bar one day with my dad when I noticed they were serving food and selling it at the counter for takeout. I asked him to order some wings to go.

When we got home, my sister and I ate the wings, and Steph said to me, "Jane, you fry wings better than they do."

"I know. I could make a lot of money if I sold my wings at one of Daddy's bars."

She was like, "Open up the old kitchen over Dauphin Street."

"Oh yeah, I can do that."

So I asked my father if I could open up the little kitchen over top of the bar. He said yes, as long as I opened up at six and shut it down by nine thirty because of school. This way, I would have time to do my homework after school and did not get to bed too late.

I had my mother take me shopping to buy large bags of whole wings and some macaroni salad. Folks did not eat wing dings at that time. We enjoyed eating the whole wing, and the macaroni salad was just a side dish. I thought the macaroni would be a great compliment and make people feel that they were getting bang for their buck. The first week was great. I made almost $300. I could not believe it. The customers seemed to like my cooking and was telling my dad that I could fry some chicken. Then I thought I would throw some fried fish into to the mix, and the customers seemed to love that as well because during the second week, I made almost $500. At the beginning of the third week, I had my mom take me shopping and load up on extra chicken and fish for the week.

The next day when my dad went in to open up the bar, someone had broken into the bar and not only stole the alcohol and beer, but had gone upstairs and stole all of the chicken, fish, and macaroni salad. They left us a note saying, "Thanks for the food."

When my dad came home and told me about the break-in and showed me the note, he was laughing while telling me that they stole the damn food too.

I was mad for about two minutes and then burst out laughing with him. *What a grateful, ornery thief,* I thought. In retrospect, I don't think anyone stole the food. I think my dad just told me that, and he actually just gave it away. I knew he did not like the fact that the older guys were spending so much time upstairs with me and bringing their cocktails upstairs while I was cooking.

My mom told me that he was getting a little upset about it.

However, that was my first taste of making money on my own terms, and I liked it.

Chapter 1

# WHO'S YOUR PARTNER?

It was March of 2017, and I was about to close one of the biggest deals of my real estate career. This was a volatile deal. These particular buyers had already walked away from the negotiations four times, so nothing was guaranteed at the table, especially my seat, which was always the first to go.

When you are about to close the deal of a lifetime, you are scared to death and somewhat numb. Why? Because you know that at any moment, your life could change financially forevermore. Or the shit could hit the fan and the deal could go right down the fucking drain, along with you finally solidifying yourself as a top-dog agent in your market. Then you realize no matter which way the pendulum swings, you have to get up and do this shit all over again, because you're only as good as your last deal!

My name is Bond, Jane Bond, and I am not a secret agent. I am a million-dollar agent! Bringing this book to fruition to share with others who are struggling, lost, and stuck real estate agents is something I have been wanting to do for quite some time.

If you are an aspiring, new, or seasoned agent who wants to learn the *who*, *what*, *when*, and *how to land your first million-dollar listing*, then this is the book for you!

At the time of writing this book, I was a broker associate at Coldwell Banker and a part of their Global Luxury Division. The Global Luxury Division is a department within the company that allows you to carry a designation of CLHMS. Yes, that's a mouthful. It stands for certified luxury home marketing specialist for agents who consistently carry million-dollar listings.

I started in real estate in 2010, and I've been a real estate agent for the past nine years. I started out selling condos for $135,000 in the crash of 2008. Now I sell and buy properties that are multi-millions of dollars for my customers on a daily basis.

I moved to Naples ten years ago after spending thirteen years in NYC as an entertainment manager, and no, not Naples, Italy—Naples, Florida. If you're like me, more than likely, you've never even heard of Naples, Florida, or knew it existed on the Gulf of Mexico.

I know some of you are thinking, what is a black girl like me, almost six feet tall with big, big hair, doing in Naples, Florida?

Believe me, I had no idea what Naples was like, or what I was going to do once I realized I was living in *Smallville* meets *Stepford Wives* with a twist. A city with zero diversity. Everyone was white, retired, wealthy, and pretty much from the Midwest.

No one looked like me. Here it was 2009, and I had never seen anything like it before. Maybe a glimmer of it in Beverly Hills.

If I had to describe Naples, it's like the Beverly Hills of the East, and the closest thing America is going to get to St. Trope.

Population of 25,000 during off season.

However, catch this! Naples is one of the wealthiest cities in the United States, and the sixth highest per capita income in the country. Naples has the second highest proportion of millionaires per capita in the United States. Our real estate is some of the most expensive in the country, and we have homes for sale in excess of $50 million on the market at any given time. How many cities can claim that?

Naples has two Ritz Carlton locations, the beach resort and the golf residence and resort.

Naples also has a large group of what you call "Quiet Luxurians." These are people who spend gobs of money to look anonymously chic.

I remember my first encounter with the neighbors. I was outside planting flowers around our massive palm tree that is shaped like a pineapple. I looked up, and this golf cart was coming up the drive, and these two people introduce themselves and asked me if I wanted to stop what I was doing and have cocktails from their cart.

In complete disbelief, I declined Ozzie and Harriet and said, "Maybe next time."

As they drove off, they waved at me, started laughing, and said, "Welcome to Naples, girlie."

Well, later I found out they were the neighborhood swingers, and were later shamed out of the community.

I also quickly learned that Naples is a destination for international wealthy vacationers, from countries such as Canada, England, and Germany. They are often looking to purchase second and third homes. They love Naples. Naples is also known for its powdery, sandy, white beaches, ninety-degree weather, boating, and luxury high-end real estate. Million-dollar condos and homes sell like hotcakes here, and that is your starting number. Hell, we had a home on the market for $88 million at one time with five acres on the beach. We will literally get into that later in the book.

We also have one of the biggest wine festivals every year, which is when I see and hear private jets flying over my head every fifteen minutes, as I sit in my office on Fifth Avenue South. It is also said that we have more private jets flying into the Naples airport than we have jets flying into Southwest Florida International Airport (RSW). Then there is the Naples Winter Wine Festival, which raises over three to five million dollars for charity, consistently every year.

Most of the women here do not work. They either golf, play tennis, go to the gym every single day, or play marjan most of the day, whatever the hell that is. Being an avid runner when I was living in NYC, I found myself trying to get into running, but it was just too damn hot and humid three quarters of the year. It is 79 to 85 degrees here four months out of the year, which is absolutely breathtaking, and 92 to 100 degrees, humid and unbearable the rest of the year. When I lived in the city, all I ever did was work, run, travel, and party. Who didn't?

After a while, I was going stir crazy just hanging out with my new husband who did not come with a manual. We will revisit that story a little later. However, my husband was starting to invest in condos, remodel them, and rent them out seasonally for an amazing amount of money, and not to mention, a great return on his investment. You know what they say, when the market is down, this is the time to invest, hold, or churn and burn.

Well, this was 2009, and the market had crashed, and Naples was hit hard, just like everywhere else in America. That's when it hit me, *I am going into the real estate business.*

If you are a new real estate agent reading this book, you're probably asking yourself, why the hell would anyone go into real estate during this time?

Because I realized it was a buyer's market. Investors and people with disposable income came from around the country and crafted incredible deals, and I wanted a ticket on that train, which was quickly pulling out of the station.

The real estate market across the country was on a spiraling downward turn, and people were rapidly losing their homes and jobs on a daily basis. All I could think of was, I had to get in the market as fast as possible. So I did my research, searching for the quickest way and best school to get my license. By May of 2010, I received my license and was off.

Every day the news was heartbreaking. Our new president, Barak Obama, had his job cut out for him. The first black president with a complete mess on his hands. The economy as a whole was doing horribly. Now it was time for me to go out and choose a broker/partner to help me build my business.

I remember looking online for real estate companies that I was familiar with from up north. However, I wanted to work in Naples, but all the companies I called that were in Naples were not interested in rookies. I was only a rookie to real estate but not life.

I remember reading one company's qualifications online, and one distinctly stood out. It stated that you had to own a luxury car, and at the time, I drove a big black Envoy, and when I turned the corner, I felt like I left the ass of the car two minutes behind me turning. I remember always being exhausted after driving that car, so with that being said, I knew that it was not going to get me in.

I also thought, *Well, shit, can I make some money first?* I had never seen something like that in writing before, a luxury car as qualification for a job.

I knew that I needed a company that had an extensive training program, with systems and tools to get me started.

Once you receive your license to sell real estate, you must hang it with a broker in order to sell real estate. I really did not understand the process of interviewing to hang my license with a firm. However, real-life experience always kicks in, and I tend to listen more than talk. I was told talking too much is telling too much, so it's best to listen. So the quest for my broker was on.

Looking at several firms, I knew right from the start that I wanted to be with a national brand. A national brand would provide me with the systems and tools that I needed to get started on my path to becoming a top agent. There were only a few of them in Naples: Weichert, Remax, Coldwell Banker, and Keller Williams. Keller Williams was not actually in Naples. They were in Bonita Springs, which was ten miles, in the other direction. Great.

The manager at Keller Williams had sent me a list of questions prior to our interview. She shared with me that the answer to all questions was "yes" when it came to Keller Williams. That's when I realized this was the company for me to start my career, and still to this day, I have relied on those very same questions and share them with every new agent I come across.

Therefore, I joined Keller Williams. The first day, I was so eager to learn everything, so I sat in this room which was staged like a bull pit for three months, listening to seasoned agents, asking a lot of questions, learning the contracts inside out, and learning how to utilize all the tools. I did not make my first sale until four months in. This is very typical of a new agent, and it can be even longer. One agent told me she did not make her first sale until after her first year of becoming an agent. I thought that definitely was not going to work for me or be me. A word to the wise, make sure you have some coins saved up before you think this is an easy gig to make lots of money. Just remember, it takes time to build up your database, understand your market, and grow your business.

A lot people think it is easy to become a real estate agent and make a lot of money. Well, it is easy to become an agent because you only have to be eighteen years old. Hell, I don't even think you have to be an American. How quickly they find out that this is hard work, a real grind, and you have to make the phone ring. A lot of agents don't realize that they are independent contractors and the CEO of their own business. While at KW, I worked really hard with buyers for sixteen months and won the Rookie of the Year award. But still I wasn't making the big dollars. I was doing volume, but nothing selling for over $200,000. After it was all said and done, my checks were anywhere from $1,900 to $2,800. Don't forget your split, taxes, and expenses have to be deducted from this money before it's all yours. I was talking to one of my colleagues, and she had just sold a $650,000 property, and I thought, *Wow, she is going to make $18,000 off that one sale, and she started at the same time I did. How is she doing this?* She told me she sat floor and got a walk-in. I'm sure the sale had nothing to do with her being single, blonde, and having big tits with quite a cute Southern belle accent. *Of course it didn't, Jane,* I told myself.

Sometimes agents sit what we call floor duty to get business. This is also called waiting around for business.

Unfortunately, that's what they do not teach you in class. You also don't know what prospecting means or how freaking unbeliev-ably boring it can be to us agents. We call it repetition boredom. Sitting two to three hours making phone calls to strangers asking if you can sell their million-dollar homes. Especially, when you are one of 7,800 realtors in a city sixteen miles long, with a population of 25,000 trying to capture the same customer. You do the math. That's 488 agents per square mile. Yes, in Naples, you could be sitting in a restaurant at any given time with twenty agents in the same restau-rant. The competition is fierce here.

It seemed like everyone I met was a realtor, or they knew some-one that was a cousin, uncle, or wife. It was incredible. I mean crazy. Even customers would get their license and become realtors just to save on the commission. Can you believe that shit? Everyone wanted in on the game.

There is a running joke here that when you get your driver's license in Naples, you also get your real estate license. Did I also mention that homeowners have no respect for the profession because they are so bombarded with agents everywhere? I was told it was completely different in the good ole days of selling real estate.

I guess that was before the crash of 2008. When everyone was making lots of money and selling lots of properties, sight unseen.

I could not even imagine buying a home for a million dollars, sight unseen, but what did I know at that time?

After winning the Rookie of the Year award, I decided to try floor duty, for once. So I was sitting one day waiting for business, and I got a call from a potential seller. OMG, I was so excited, until the conversation went like this:

"Ma'am, I think I can get more money for my place because I have done many upgrades and it is a double wide, not a single."

Okay, you have to imagine my face. I was sitting there thinking, *What the hell is he talking about?* So said, "Excuse me, could you repeat that, sir?"

He repeated the words, "A double wide."

I said, "I'm sorry, sir, I'm not familiar with that term."

He said, "You never heard of a double-wide trailer?"

I thought, *What?* I asked him, "Could you hold on for a minute, please, sir?" Call it what you want, but I never picked the call back up. The next week I left KW for good.

Sotheby's had opened up an office in Naples, and I had told my husband if Sotheby's ever opened an office here in Naples, I was going to do everything in my power to work under their flag.

Two weeks later, I interviewed with Sotheby's broker, Christopher Harrington, and he and I got along like a house on fire.

At the time, I did not know that the office I interviewed with was the top-grossing office in all of Florida. Agents were calling and asking me how I got in that office as a rookie. I simply said that I was interviewed and was asked to join. I must say, it was quite glamourous and had a nice ring to it to say I worked for Sotheby's Broad Avenue office at the time. I really did not know much about Sotheby's real estate arm, only that it was a big name in NYC as far as the auction house was concerned. Funny enough, I lived around the corner from the auction house on the upper eastside when I lived in NYC, and there was always an amazing story in the *New York Times* about some wealthy person purchasing an expensive piece of art, jewelry, rug, or antique from them for major money. They even had a section called Mansion Global with nothing but mansions for sale all around the world.

Therefore, I knew they already had the clientele to purchase not only million-dollar homes, but multimillion-dollar homes.

I also noticed later on that agents from other companies were intimidated or envious of you when you came across them. It was really funny because this particular office had agents with celebrity names such Phil Collins, Michael Jordan, Patricia Fields, and of course, Jane Bond. It was a new start, and I was able to up my game because once some of the big agents met me and got to know me, I was able to sit their open houses for their million-dollar listings. Also, the branding and marketing tools were beautiful and worthy of million-dollar listings. I remember thinking, *Why did it take me so long to get here? Uh, because you were chasing your tail and had no idea what the hell you were doing, Jane.* All the agents drove Mercedes, Porsches, and Jaguars, which was very impressive. Thank God I had gotten rid of my gigantic clunker of Envoy and bought a little GLK Mercedes 250 before making the move. Talking about needing to fit in.

So the day before I started at the new office, there was a sales meeting at the *Naples Daily News* building for all of the Sotheby's agents to talk about changes to the Naples Board of Realtors Contract, also called the NABOR Contract. Let's not forget, I was working in Bonita Springs at KW, which was in Lee County, and Naples was in Collier County, the preferred county, little did I know. So I pulled up in my little black GLK with my new signage on my rear window, which was a picture of my face and the top half of my body that covered the whole entire rear window with all my information on it, proud because I was a Sotheby's agent. I go into the meeting and everyone was there, including all these familiar faces I had seen in the magazines selling million-dollar properties. I felt like all eyes were on me as walked in. There had to be at least three hundred agents there because this was a mandatory meeting. Even Judy Greene was there, who was the head honcho of Southwest Florida Sotheby's. To my surprise, she knew who I was and came right up to me to welcome me to the company. I felt great, and then I looked around, and I was the only black face in the entire room. I thought, *Oh my, am I the only black person in the company, in all of Florida?* Then the meeting began, and the first thing they started speaking about was branding. On a big screen, they were pointing out the dos and don'ts of branding, and everyone was laughing at the illustrations. I was also laughing, until I saw an illustration that mirrored the big ad that I so ridiculously had in the rear window of my car.

I became mortified.

I was sure some of the agents saw me pull up in my little black GLK with this humongous picture of me in the rear window of my car. I must have looked like I had seen a ghost because I stopped laughing right at that illustration, and embarrassment began to set in. I could not wait to get out of there before anyone could see me in my car. So I acted like I had to go to the restroom and slipped out of the meeting, only to run into Christopher Harrington, my new broker in the parking lot. He asked me why I was leaving so soon as he peered at my rear window.

He started smiling and said, "I know why." He started to laugh and walked away at the same time, yelling back at me, "I will see you tomorrow, Jane Bond, at the office."

I just wanted to sit there and cry, but I thought I better leave before some snooty agent came out and saw me and told everyone about my sign. I thought, *Damn it, he saw me before could get away.* I could not get to the sign company fast enough to tell them to take that horrific ass signage off my car. I won't tell you that it was my husband's bright idea and I was against it the whole time, but you know, ladies, we are always trying to please them too, even when we know it's the wrong move sometimes.

I knew the shit was whacked from the start. Even some of my friends came forward after I removed it and said that they thought it was kinda cheap and tacky but didn't want to tell me. Can you imagine if I had showed up at the office with that sign on my car?

All I can say is that somebody was looking out for me. I would have been the laughingstock of the office.

Welcome to the unbelievable world of million-dollar listings, where the competition is fierce. But no need to worry, agents. Competition is healthy. It breeds champions. Therefore, all you have to do is decide if you want to be a champion in this business.

Landing your first million-dollar listing is about competing with some of the best agents in your market to get the job done.

Today's customers, whether they're millennials or baby boomers, want the same thing: an experience when selling or buying a home with an agent. Dealing with customers of a certain financial status takes some understanding of who these customers are, what they do, what they have in common, and why they only want the best.

I decided after two years into my career that I wanted to be one of the best, if not *the* best in my market.

Chapter 2

......................................

# MY BIG WHY

I had not yet discovered my *big why*. This might seem very cliché, until you receive the phone call I received one day from my mother, which was pretty disturbing.

She had gotten stuck in her bathtub and couldn't get out. She tried to climb out and fell out and, of course, hurt herself. It was like that commercial from the emergency alert people: I have fallen and I can't get up. Well, that was my mother. When she fell out of the tub, there was nobody around to help her, and on top of that, she started getting vertigo. Vertigo refers to a sense of spinning dizziness. It is a symptom of a range of condition that stops her in her tracks and causes her to throw up.

Being three hours away from my mother by plane and not being able to do anything to help her terrified me, and on top of that, she was alone at the time.

Finally, after a few hours, I was able get someone to come and help her by kicking the door in. Now, here it was, I was faced with a couple of harsh realities that needed to be taken care of immediately.

One, I had a mother who has heart disease, and I needed to make sure her home was designed properly, specifically the bathroom, so that she could grow old in her home and be able to bathe properly as an elderly woman. Two, how in the hell was I going to remedy this so it would never happen again and make sure she was safe?

I knew I had no other choice but to make something happen. Also, asking my siblings was out of the question because they didn't have the extra income to help me financially with this. So I had to figure out a way to make this happen sooner rather than later.

This was when my *big why* became crystal clear to me. All I could think about, day in and day out, was that I had to do something about this situation, and that was what fueled me. I found myself not eating healthy, not sleeping, going in and out of a mild state of depression, always in a bad mood, and very desperate for a solution.

Understanding my *big why* made me put my foot on the gas and keep moving. I decided this was it. If I was going to be in this game of high-stakes real estate, then I was going to go for it full fucking speed ahead and *no looking back, Jane. You will no longer be a secret agent. I will become a million-dollar agent* was what told myself for the last time. One day, I received an invitation from a mortgage broker who shared with me that I had to come and hear this man speak about real estate and that I was a great candidate for his course. I thought, *Here we go. Another sales pitch, and what is she getting out of this?* I had nothing to lose, so I took her up on her offer and went the next day.

I had gone to a couple of real estate seminars in the past, but this speaker was different. He was tall, slightly handsome, very sharply dressed, with a commanding voice of confidence, and in your face. One of his very first questions to the audience was how did some of us travel to the event. He then proceeded to tell us that he came in his Rolls-Royce Ghost. I thought, *Ooh shit, okay*! Then he talked about being professionally dressed when you come to events like this, and not like you're going to the beach wearing shorts and sandals. He called out a couple of the attendees for dressing this way. That was when I perked up because I thought this was going to be good and I was big on being professionally dressed and showing up properly. Maybe this came from living in NYC and knowing every time you leave out of your door in the city, you must be on point because you never know who you're going to run into or meet. This was a part of your NYC bible—always be on! He proceeded to talk to us about money and how much we were possibly making a year. He was breaking it down, telling us it was shameful that most of us in the room probably only made $40,000, if that, in any given year because we were lazy and did not know how to commit to our business, which was customer service.

He told the audience that we should be making at least $250,000 to a million dollars a year in our business. Then of course, here came the sales pitch for the coaching course. He also said that he could teach us how to make a million dollars a year if we just followed his system for a whopping $13,000, if we signed up today.

That was two years prior to this happening to my mother.

Me being the skeptic that I am, I clearly did not believe him at that time or believe in myself enough to pursue the offer to gain the skill set and knowledge. Nor did I have the money. I just thought it was another scam to get damn money.

Fast-forward twenty-four months later, and I was still chasing my tail like so many other realtors. Running behind buyers posing as a taxi service and praying someone, anyone of these buyers would pull the damn trigger and purchase a house. Not even really qualifying them, but just going on hope and prayer.

I remember taking one buyer out, and she brought along her little dog. Unbeknownst to me, she fed him egg salad in nine-ty-nine-degree weather. When I stepped away from the car to open the property up for her, the dog had vomited all over my console. In between everything was freakin' dog puke. I could not believe it!

She kept apologizing but never one time did she offer or ask me if I wanted her to pay to have my car detailed.

Another time, I showed this buyer fifteen houses in one day. One after another, which was crazy of me. Being Miss Pleaser, and the fact that she told me she had to move quickly because of family issues, I did it. Well, needless to say, she had the nerve to call me and tell me that her family issue had come full circle and that they were upset at her because she did not hire her cousin, who was just start-ing out in the business, and that she had to continue her search with him. Of course, I found out later she bought one of the properties

I showed her and purchased it through her cousin. Oh, and did I forget to mention she was a friend?

Wrong, so wrong! I think my worst experience, though, was when I took this family out, and every time we would go out, the whole family would come. Three bad ass boys, a screaming little girl, mother, father, and both sets of in-laws. Crazy, right?

I never understood why they would all come along. It wasn't like the in-laws were going to live with them. I guess they had to approve of the property.

The boys would go into each home and wreak havoc. They would jump on the beds, throw pillows around, and run outside. To make things worse, the little girl knocked over a glass vase to get attention, then started screaming at top of her lungs. I was standing there in a state of shock with my mouth wide open the first time this happened. The second time we went out was even more horrible. The in-laws got into a heated argument because the boys started fighting and knocked the little girl into the pool. When she came up, her nose was bloody, and all hell broke loose. I was totally outdone.

Can you imagine this whole scene? Needless to say, I never saw them again. I thought, *What the hell is going on with these buyers I'm getting?* Then I think there has to be a light at the end of this very dark tunnel. The next night, my husband told me we were going out to dinner with friends of ours from England who were selling their home here in Naples, and I thought, *Wow, this is my chance to finally get a listing*.

Well, I thought wrong. Not only did I not get the listing, I got my feelings hurt and somewhat insulted that I wasn't even in the running for the listing. The husband simply told me in his own snide way, "Look us up when you start selling million-dollar listings like this well-known agent in the city."

I will never forget how that put a baseball in my throat coming from him. I can still feel that moment as I write the words on this page.

I knew it had to be a better way, and I was definitely going to figure it out after that night for the sake of my sanity and mother.

I was also tired of seeing the same usual suspects on the boards. You're probably asking yourself, what boards? Those damn boards that hung so proudly in the hall or in the supply room of your office. At Sotheby's, our broker hung them in the passageway to upstairs. I could not get past it without seeing it because my office was on the second floor.

It had all the agents, new and pending listings, and sales. I would walk by this board every day and think, *How can I get my name on both sides of those damn boards every month?* Of course, it was always in your face and a horrible daily reminder that you truly were a secret agent. An agent with no business and did not know when or where your next customer was going to come from.

I'm sure if you're reading this book, you have been there. Having no business as a real estate agent and not knowing where the next customer is coming from is a scary thought, especially with bills to pay each and every month. I felt like I was dying because I am a fighter and a survivor. I did not want this to beat me.

Like an idiot, I would add up the enormous amounts of commissions of the top producing agents, somebody else's money, which were the same top ten agents in my office. And boy did they make a lot of money on a monthly basis.

For two agents in particular, one was making at least $300,000 a month consistently, carrying no more than twelve to fifteen listings at a time, well worth over $150 million in listings. I thought, *My god, I will never get there, no way on earth.* She worked in the Port Royal area of Naples only. This is where the wealthiest people of Naples lived. Homes in Port Royal could cost anywhere from six million to eighty-eight million, especially on Gordon Drive, which is all beach-front. You also get to belong to the Port Royal Club.

She was the reigning queen down there, and being blonde, six feet tall, and a size six didn't hurt either. She was also number 131 of the top 250 agents in the country. I don't think she ever left Port Royal. That was her farm. She had one assistant who did not talk to anyone much at all. At first, I thought it was strange. However, looking back now as I was growing my business, I totally understood how important it is to have a support system like that.

For those who don't know what a farm is or the term *farming*, it's just what it sounds like. It's where you stay in one area or community and you become an expert there. Learning everything you can about the area or community, inside and out. Sometimes I would see her on CNBC. I was also told that the national papers would call on her often for quotes about the market. Now that's when you know your shit, and it can be quite glamorous to be on TV. I admired and envied her at the same time. However, my envy was always blue because envy comes in all shades. Blue envy is wanting to be looked at in the same vein.

The other agent was a few years younger than I was and was a spitting image of Cameron Diaz. She was tall, blonde, very pretty, confident, and funny. She was also clocking in at $50,000 to $70,000 a month. I thought, *How in the hell are they consistently doing this?* She was lovely, though, and friendly toward me. We worked on the same floor and would often speak about life and marriage. She did not want to get married, and the guys she had dated in the past just did not seem strong enough for her. I believe she hated selling real estate but loved making the big dollars, and that she did. She always talked to me about leaving Naples and doing something else she often expressed her love for. Rehabbing million-dollar properties. I think she just had a love-hate relationship with real estate, as we all do.

She always spoke to me about the business being such a grind, but she was doing amazing and would always say if she left, where would she make this kind of money anywhere else.

It was our broker Christopher Harrington's birthday party, and they were throwing him a surprise party at a restaurant. We decided to go together. While there, I shared with her over cocktails that I was sick and tired of chasing my tail and that I had to do something because of my mother.

I told her that I had gone to this seminar, a couple of years back, where I met and listened to the speaker who said that I could make a million dollars a year in this business. I started laughing.

She looked at me very seriously and said, "You can. I do, and I'm on track for this year."

Then she proceeded to say she had been coaching with him for several years now.

I looked her dead in her eyes and said, "You're fucking kidding me."

She said, "No, Jane, I'm very serious, and I'm not the only one."

She started naming other agents, and they were making close to a million a year too from being coached by this guy. And I knew it was true because idiot me was adding up their sales at times wishing it was me.

I turned to her and said, "I am signing up tomorrow."

She said, "You go, girl."

After that conversation and a couple more drinks, all I could think of is, *Where in the hell am I going to get this money from?*

If I remembered correctly, the price was $13,000 a year, two years ago.

Chapter 3

# WHEN THE LIGHTS CAME ON

The next morning with a clear head, I started playing the records back of that day two years ago. I remember him saying to us that our goal as agents should be to achieve a repeatable, duplicatable business, which would give us the lifestyle we could only dream of. That meant to me that I could take care of my mother and also have my husband's back if we ever came up on some serious money issues. So I decided to take on the coach. I knew I had what it took to make it in this business. I just needed to know exactly what to do and be held accountable. At the seminar, he told us just that. He spoke about prospecting, cold calling, lead generating, and where these leads came from. He also shared with us the tools that we would need to do the job and that all we had to do was be consistent with calling and following up on good leads.

He said after ninety days, it would all come together and we would see a change in our business. That was good enough for me. I really could not afford it at the time, but I gave it a shot and put it on my credit card without even sharing it with my husband. I figured if I sold one $500,000 home, that would pay off the coaching for the year, and hopefully, I would learn something in the process too. So I started putting my plan together.

I will never forget how excited I was to get started. It was like a voracious hunger I could not wait to fill. I remember calling and asking when was my sales kit going to arrive and when was my coach going to reach out to me. All I could think about was making a million dollars to take care of things. However, I was not prepared for the amount of work and commitment that lay ahead of me.

It was August 2014 when I received my coach's e-mail introducing himself along with his credentials. I remember being scared and excited at the same time while reading through his accolades, thinking this guy was no bullshit. He had worked for the motivational king, Tony Robbins, taking a sales division in his company from over $3.5 million in sales to just under $9 million in sales in less than thirteen months! He also worked with the likes of Brian Tracy, Lou Holtz, Pat Riley, General Norman Schwarzkopf, and many other great thought leaders. In addition, he worked in the field of sports psychology and mental toughness, working with people like tennis pros Pete Sampras and Monica Seles, and golfer Ernie Els. I thought, *Holy shit, I will not be able to feed this guy any of my lazy bullshit.* It did not matter. I was going to do whatever it took to make this work. Nor did I forget that I just put thirteen thousand dollars on my credit card and did not tell my husband. So I had to make this work to pay off my card. Not to mention, my $3,340 monthly mortgage payment and $50,000 of credit card debt that had nothing to do with my new husband, and now the $13,000 on top of that. I was completely running out of my savings each month and desperate.

Even though I was only paying the minimum on my cards, I still could not get ahead because of the interest. To make things worse, once I decided to sell my house, that took almost two years. I was just paying the mortgage on something I was not using. And finally the worst scenario. My mother needing me to help her and I couldn't.

So there was no turning back, no giving in, or giving up. I had to succeed and learn how to become a million-dollar listing agent.

The next day, I received another e-mail from my coach which contained two blank business plans. One for the previous year and one for the upcoming year. I remember being so embarrassed while reading through the series of questions in reference to my numbers.

It was clear to me at that moment that I had no idea what my numbers were or what the hell I had been doing for past two years. What I did realize was that I had been chasing my tail with no direction and this was a direct route to success. Looking at the structure of the business plan, I knew if I just applied myself ten-fold, I could win.

Even though we were told we could make a million dollars in a year, I was still a skeptic, and I was not a hundred percent confident in my skill set as of yet. But I knew I was hungry enough, and this was my chance to at least give it my best damn shot! Taking another look at this business plan with different eyes, I was able to understand the way it worked. So I started filling out the business plan with a recap from my previous year's production: (1) total income paid $52,333.20, (2) total expenses $6,729.00, (3) closed deals, (4) listing appointments, (5) I started talking to myself asking questions like, *How could you even think you could make money, Jane? Looking at these numbers you're putting down, what exactly were you doing at work all day long, girl?* and (6) two words came to my mind: *lazy ass*.

Next question: average list price, $629,000; average commission check, $8,600; average hours worked, forty hours a week; present pending, zero; present inventory, five listings; days worked, five; total hours prospecting, no answer; and last total contacts, no answer. I could not answer these last questions because I did not track my business. Therefore, I could not gauge from the previous year where, when, or who my business came from. Big mistake and very first lesson learned: *tracking your business*. By not tracking my business, I had no pipeline, and it cost me two years of building my business. Now it came time to project for the next year and I was still not sure of my skill set. So I thought if I put down $200,000 and achieve it, I would at least pay off my credit card bills, help my mom, and still make quite a bit of money. So I started doing the math. Sixteen deals in one year with an average selling price of $630,000 would gross me over $10,000,000 for the year. I thought, *Wow! I could do that! It does not seem so far-fetched, Jane.* I continued, $10,000,000 gross production is $300,000 in gross commission income with a split of 80/20, and a 6% royalty off the top.

I would walk away easily with $227,404.80. By writing it out and seeing it in front of me for the first time, I knew I could do it.

The next day, I woke up at 5:30 a.m. and started working out.

My husband was shocked. He was like, "You have never gotten up at five thirty in the morning, unless we were flying off somewhere."

I told him I just felt energized and ready to take on the world. I could not wait to get out of bed and get to work. It was like something came over me and I needed to capture every minute of the day to get everything in. I worked out every day that week and the next. I found myself going to the gym five days a week so I could keep my energy up and sleep well at night. I also changed my diet to only having one glass of wine at dinner, a gallon of water a day, and more fish than meat, which also gave me more energy during the course of the week. I always kept an itinerary, but I felt as though I needed a new one to go with my new attitude and mind-set. I remember writing out my week. Rise up at 5:30 a.m., work out till 6:30 a.m., shower and dressed by 7:30 a.m., check last evening and morning e-mails on the phones by 8:00 a.m., role-playing, and by 8:30 a.m., hardcore prospecting till 11:30 am. Little did I know that this was my life five days a week for next three years.

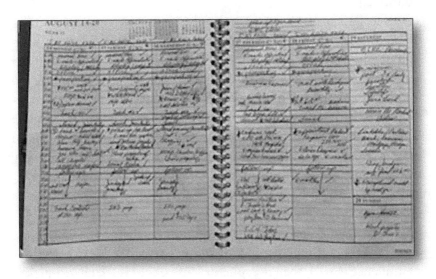

Once I received my sales kit in the mail with all the scripts, CDs, and tracking sheets to track my business, it was a go.

My husband was telling everyone, "My wife is going for it. I can see it in her eyes. All she does is get up, go to work, come home, and continue to work."

He had never been so right about me or seen me wanting something so badly. Like I said earlier, it was like a voracious hunger and an unquenchable thirst to learn everything about winning in this business. I downloaded all the CDs in my car so I could listen to them every time I was driving to and from work, and anytime in between. There was no more listening to the radio, only the CDs to get me to the next level. You would have thought I was an actress learning her scripts for a big movie role. I practiced every evening at home, before and after dinner. I had my husband roleplay with me as if he was the customer. The fire was lit, and I was feeling it!

At the same time, I started getting my database in order, pulling all my past clients together in its own category (PC). Next, my center of influence (COI), then my sphere of influence (SOI), cherry-picked expired listings, and anybody that might give me a business category.

This allowed me to be better organized when I started prospecting.

Then, I purchased my very first dialer system, and it was like the lights all of sudden came on for the first time in my career. I thought, *Holy shit!* It was called MOJO, a hands-free system that could dial up to sixty-five numbers an hour without hearing a ring, so you had to be ready as soon as you heard the prospect say hello and you were on.

I thought, *Game on!* I also bought a Bluetooth earpiece, which enabled me the mobility to move around and not feel confined. It also heightened my enthusiasm while engaging with prospective customers over the phone. It finally all made sense and tied everything together for me. Now I understood how I was going to be able to track my business and grow it exponentially. *YASSS!* I thought.

By going after expired listings on a daily basis, it made perfect sense that these were the customers that needed me the most, because their property had not sold during season for whatever reason. I was able to lead generate, follow up, keep great notes, and send out thank-you cards to what we called hot leads. A hot lead is any prospect that is ready to sell in the next thirty days. It took me two weeks to learn my scripts. I learned the expired script and all the objections. Looking back on my first few times calling, I totally sucked. I mean sucked!

Stuttering and not feeling confident—it was bad, but I kept going. I shared an office with two other agents at the time, and it felt very uncomfortable trying to make my calls with them in the room.

I was still a rookie at Sotheby's and the only African American in the highest-grossing office in all of Southwest Florida. So of course, I felt had something to prove. I went to my broker Christopher Harrington, whom I adored and got along with like a house on fire and explained to him my issue of needing privacy while pretty much dialing for dollars. He completely understood and told me to come up with a solution, so I did. We had a closet in the office that I shared, and I had him pretty much turn it into a prospecting room for me. If you can imagine this, the closet was as small as a phone booth. I cleaned all the mess out, painted it white, nailed a whiteboard to the wall, and added a mirror and a dock to hang my scripts behind me, so I could flip through them as I made calls.

Every day for the next 90 to 120 days, I came into work at 7:30 a.m., got started at 8:00 a.m., role-played for fifteen to twenty minutes, and then hit the phones for three steady straight hours. With ten-minute breaks every forty-five minutes, it was like being in a tunnel for three hours. I am not going to lie, it was not fun. However, I started noticing something around the forty-five-day mark.

I was becoming good at this prospecting stuff and able to capture the prospect's attention. The hang-ups were becoming few and far in between. Some customers I called back even remembered me by name, not that my name wasn't memorable. They were starting to have full-on conversations with me.

Some conversations were too long and not business generating but a great confidence builder.

I started studying the market more carefully, checking the stats daily on the MLS sells, expireds, pending, and new listings. I almost did not recognize myself. I was becoming a machine. I knew exactly what I was talking about and could back it up. I memorized all the objections and could take anyone on. I was consistent with my follow-up, which realized later was the brass ring. And if that was the brass, then you all know what the platinum was of course. The appointment, the presentation baby! Showtime! The listing presentation.

I will never forget the first listing appointment I booked from prospecting. It was like the skies opened up and angels started singing.

I can remember it like it was yesterday. I got to the home thirty minutes early, parked my car around the corner, and started practicing the scripts. I was nervous as hell. Then, the time came for me to go and present to the customer. Even though I had been calling prospects for at least sixty days straight, I was a nervous wreck walking into the home.

This was a $850,000-dollar-listing appointment, the most expensive appointment I had ever gone on. Remember, prior to this, all the properties I had ever listed were $600,000 and under.

I remember walking into the home, exchanging hellos, and feeling like I was a fish in a fishbowl. The wife was giving me the once-over, as well as the husband, the dog, and the kids. I did not know what to make of it at first, so I broke the ice by taking a quick look around and sharing with them how lovely their home was. Then I asked if they would mind if I took a look around the entire house before we got started. They seemed very happy with my suggestion. The wife started pointing out all the upgrades they had done to the home in the past year, which was great information to ascertain. As I walked through the home with her, I shared with her how beautiful I thought her home was and that she had done a wonderful job with the space. I also told her that I was a former interior designer and understood the bones of her home. I also told her that I had designed the homes of several dignitaries and pro-athletes all over the country. Her husband was very impressed when I dropped a few names. This really started meshing the conversation together along with the next steps to unfolding the presentation. Boom! I was winning, but something happened at the end of the presentation that I did not expect. They did not sign the contract.

They kindly said it was nice meeting me and that they were interviewing other agents and would get back to me. That was when my daily training kicked in and the lightbulb immediately came on. *This is an objection, Jane, live and in living color.* So I turned to the customer and boldly asked what was their hesitation on signing the contract with me that day. They simply said that they had made appointments with other agents and wanted to honor them. I did not have a comeback after that. And I definitely did not want to seem desperate, even though I was. Funny enough, though, I did not feel defeated or like I failed. It was actually the opposite. I felt like I had won! Why? Because I just nailed my first formal presentation, and I felt like I was ready to take on any of the three personalities in this business, especially the analytical one, which is usually the most challenging.

# Chapter 4

........................................

# YOUR CUSTOMER OR YOUR MONEY

There are three personalities in this business you come across. The *driver* who likes to be in control. The *analytical* wants nothing but the facts. The *expressive* who is usually the life of the party and likes to talk a lot. You can barely get him off the phone when prospecting. Sometimes it's a nice break to get an expressive on the phone because the daily rejection can be hard. However, being rejected so many times a day somehow makes you stronger. It seemed like once I stopped being emotional about it and not taking it personal, I was able to find empathy in their anger by siding with them and sharing with them that I would not call them ever again and that would do everything in my power to get them off the list, even though I could not do anything about it. The lesson here is: it is better to be empathetic as opposed to emotional, which most of the times ensues into an argument with the customer.

The analytical customer is the one you really need to know your shit with, or he will definitely call you out, or you simply will never hear from him again.

I find it very interesting when you internalize something and bring passion to it, you become good at it, you build confidence, and you are able to articulate it with expertise because you have put everything into the process. After that experience with my first presentation, I could not wait to get back on the phones to make more appointments.

I knew from tracking my numbers that I should be going on at least three to four appointments a week. I was not there yet. However, I felt it coming.

The next week, I had already set up two appointments and two for the following week. Now, I was coming up on the ninety-day mark and twelve one-on-one calls with my coach. I remember feeling exhausted and sharing with my coach that I had never worked so hard before in my life. Between the daily three hours of calling, follow-up, packaging and mailing out prelisting marketing info, and handwriting at least five to ten personal thank-you cards after every good lead, doing this day in and day out was pretty grueling as a single agent. I had no assistant. It was all on me, and I had a lot riding on this whole process.

I would get home around 6:30 pm., have a bite to eat, and continue to work.

I mean it was intense. I would go out to dinner with my husband and fall asleep at the table. I was so tired, but nothing was going to stop me. The very next day, I got the call that I was waiting for.

Lo and behold, my very first appointment I went on three weeks prior called.

The customers that gave me the once-over were actually on the phone sharing with me how impressed they were with my knowledge of the market and felt like I represented exactly what they wanted in a realtor. They wanted to sign with me as their listing agent. I could not believe my ears. All I could think of in my mind was *SCORED*!

I had already written them off, and it was like the heavens opened up and won the lottery. My first big win was a $850,000 listing. Finally, I broke through and got past the $650,000 mark. I could not believe it. I was on cloud nine. It worked! Ninety days and I saw my business actually turning around. The next week, I got another listing for $975,000 and another one for, wait for it, $1,300,000! I saw it all coming together, and I was like a freight train speeding down the track, collecting listings left and right. I looked up and had twenty-five listings. I did not recognize myself.

Everything my coach told me had come to fruition. I thought, *Now the work begins.*

I brought on my first staff member, an assistant/buyer's agent. She was very pretty and smart. She was really good with graphic design and helped me with marketing of all the listings and reshaping the office.

I had finally come out of the fucking closet so to speak, emerging like super-fucking-woman. I remember listening to Alicia Keys' song "I Am Your Super Woman" on my computer every day and trying to be just that, wearing a cape every day to fly. I made it, but it was exciting and scary at the same time.

My new assistant and I worked well together because she was just as excited as I was and was new to the business and at Sotheby's. I was now working with an agent on her way up, which is looked at in our business as lucky, to get in on the ground floor with an agent on her way up to becoming a top agent. I never got that opportunity. Maybe in retrospect, the writing was on the wall and a top agent said to herself, *I'm not going to bring her on because she is too hungry.* It can definitely be looked at as a threat to some agents in the business.

I went to my broker and told him that I needed the entire office to work more efficiently, and he agreed. So he found a place for the other two agents to store their files, because they barely came to the office anyway.

On the other hand, I was in the office every morning at seven thirty and needed the privacy. So we went to work on rearranging the office to be more conducive to my new work environment, as an agent on my way to the top. I decided to mimic the Camren Diaz look-alike agent's office. She had a nice-looking office, all-white modern furniture, and lovely artwork. What was special was, she had an entire wall painted with erasable paint so she could track her business. I thought that was so cool.

So I copied her and painted one side of our office's entire wall with erasable paint too. Therefore, I could watch each listing transaction unfold by its timeline from start to finish. She would even come by and go, "Wow, I can't believe you did it." It felt really good to be recognized for my work ethic. The wall was filled with the timeline of each listing: Date listing was taken, date it went under contract, inspection scheduled, initial escrow collected, date of financing contingency waived, date inspection period was over, when contract went hard, final walk-through, and closing date. I had $22 million in listings up on the wall. It was one of the most amazing days of my career to witness. Can you image in ninety days, I went from five listings to twenty-five listings worth $22 million? Come on now, you got to give it to your girl. That was what hard work, perseverance, your *big why*, and a lot of tears will do for ya!

And I had only just started to scratch the surface of my business. Little did I know what lay ahead of me.

We started the marketing wheel, sending out an e-mail blast throughout the company, informing all internal and external agents of any new listings that came in. I also had five listings rotating every week in the local paper, the *Florida Weekly*'s open-house section, which was free. Everyone read it, especially the tourists. It told you everything that was going on in Naples on a weekly basis and gave me quite a bit of exposure.

I would see people I knew, and they would say to me, "I saw all your listings in the paper, and it looks like you're doing well, Jane," and that felt great.

We decided that instead of bringing on a showing agent, we would create an open-house schedule and roll it out to all the agents in the office that could sit open house, because the two of us could not handle them all. This was brilliant. This way we could have at least six or seven open houses at one time, on any given Sunday. Then she and I would go around and make sure the sitting agent locked up properly. It was a good system. We also created an information booklet for each listing, so the sitting agents would know everything about the property, and all the information was right there at their fingertips. We asked that they did not remove it from the property. It never dawned on me that we were creating our own systems and tools at that time, which was great until some agents started calling out at the last minute. Then it became chaos trying to cover the property at the last minute. I always say be careful what you wish for.

Something weird was starting to happen, though, and I was starting to get really nervous. Thirty days had passed, and then another three weeks. Nothing was going under contract. I thought,

*This cannot be happening to me. Nothing is selling.* I started getting depressed, thinking, *Could I have done all this work, getting all of these listings, and I'm not going to be able sell any of them? It's freaking January, the height of the season, and none of them are moving off the wall.* At that moment, I realized getting the listing is one thing. Selling them is another.

So I started going out networking with people, being seen at different functions, engaging with other agents, sharing information about my listings, and talking to them about theirs. As I was gathering information, I told my assistant to prepare a list of the top agents' listings and open houses for me each week, and I would make my rounds so that they could see me on the scene also being proactive. I started to engage with other top agents from other companies by showing up at their listings, and of course, I would always be dressed well. That's one thing I pride myself on—always looking good, smelling good, and dressing well. I noticed that a lot of these agents that had big listings drove beautiful, expensive cars but dressed casually or even cheaply, which was beyond me. I thought to myself, *If I had those type of listings, I would not only drive one of the hottest cars, but I would also dress like a superstar agent. Nails, feet, hair, clothes, bags, and shoes would be on point.*

That's what success looks like for me at a certain level.

If I'm going to carry 50 to 100 million dollars in listings, then I'm damn sure going to look like a million dollars!

As I continued to show up at these top agents' listings, looking amazing on a regular basis, they started taking note and asking me to go out with them sometime for lunch or coffee. One even said she could possibly have a buyer for one of my listings. The next week, I got a call from that agent, and two weeks later, I was under contract with my first million-dollar listing, $1.3 million, an all-cash deal.

We went out to dinner that night after the closing, and she just poured all this information into me about how she became a top listing agent. She shared with me that she had drove all the way from Boston with $376 in her pocket and was not sure if she had a place to live but had met this guy while he was visiting Boston in the summer.

He told her she could live with him in Naples for six months, free of charge, but after that, she had to leave because his roommate would be coming back from Australia.

So she said she took him up on his offer and packed up her horrible little life in Boston, which was going nowhere anyway, and took a chance. It panned out for her because the guy came through.

She told me if she stayed in Boston, she would have ended up dead or in Alcoholics Anonymous. I did not press on for details, but I knew it had something to do with a man.

She knew she only had six months to sink or swim. So she took a waitressing job, got her real estate license, and started telling everybody she met that she sold real estate on the side until she could go full-time. A nice couple walked in one day and struck up a conversation with her. She told them her story, and they shared with her that they had friends moving to Naples who were looking for a new home and maybe she could help them out when they arrived. They asked for her information and said they would give it to their friends. She said three months had passed by and she never heard from them again. In the fourth month, she received a call from the friends, and they explained to her that they had to change their plans and were ready to come to Naples and asked if she would still be available to help them. They told her that their friends had spoken very highly of her friendliness, customer service, and attentiveness. To make a long story short, she sold them a 5.5 million-dollar house, and the rest was history.

However, she said she never forgot those three words: friendliness, customer service, and attentiveness, and she has lived by this ever since.

She told me, "Give them the best of you with service and attention, Jane, and you will always win."

Of course, my inner confidence kicked in, and I thought, *I'm gonna win anyway, no matter what it takes. Because I have what it takes.*

We all have what it takes inside of us. We just have to find our fire and walk through it! There is no room for failure, and at this time in my life, it is just unacceptable. Knowing like her, I have no other choice at this time in my life, and my life needed desperately to change. Because of my mother and myself, I was on and going for the platinum ring.

Screw the gold! Ajani Scott of VH1's *Love & Listings* recently shared with me, "Success does not happen overnight, but it can happen in one night," and I was definitely in need of it happening in one night.

Something else the agent shared with me that I did not know. She told me that I was the talk of the town among agents and they were watching what I was doing and wondering how it was happening so fast for me.

In spite of this news, I took it with a grain of salt because it did not feel like things were happening so quickly for me. I just did the work, which I thought was pretty grueling.

I knew that I had to keep pushing, marketing, and filling up my pipeline with listings. Because as one sold, I had to replace it with another listing to keep the momentum going. So I did not stop going into the closet making calls. The routine had to stay in place because had become very results driven at this point, and anything less did not work for me.

Season was in full bloom, and people had come to Naples to get away from the cold. The traffic got increasingly heavy, the restaurants completely packed out, hotel and beaches were full, and people were everywhere.

As agents, we love season. Wealthy Canadians, Germans, and English citizens travel across the world to come to Naples to get away from the cold.

Americans that come from up North and the Midwest to get away all fall in love with Naples and buy real estate on impulse.

My phone did not stop ringing. We had showings every day, and I was still going on presentations. Between the presentation showings, open houses, and still prospecting, I was going crazy. We were on call constantly. Listings were going under contract left and right, which came along with inspections and following up with bank financing and attorneys. I was actually running a full-service real estate business.

I had become the CEO of the Bond Group. It was real, not something I had just put a title on. It was working full on. I looked up at the wall one day, and eight of our listing were under contract, five had recently closed, and we still had seven listings, along with three coming in for over a million dollars each. I had become a million-dollar listing agent within six months, after five years as an agent. Now when I look back, I think, *what the hell was I doing for the past four years in my career?* What a difference six months can make in your life if you focus and become accountable for your actions within the process.

# Chapter 5

........................................

# THE REALIZATION

Working with maximum efficiency and staying completely focused on prospecting and customer service, I earned $375,000. More money than I had ever earned in my life in any one year.

Some people don't make this type of money in a lifetime. This is some high-powered executive money. Oh, wait a minute, I am a CEO, boss bitch, lady of my own business. Here it is, in six to eight months, I made CEO money with a lot of believing in myself, long talks to myself, affirmations, the universe aligning the stars, me being open to allow all this to happen, and not without the grace of God! When you believe in yourself and ask the universe for what you want and then be open to law of allowing, you have just activated the laws of attraction.

Ask and it is given.

I called my mother every other day, but this particular day was going to be different! When she picked up the phone, I asked how her day was going and if she was alone.

She replied, "Yes. You sound different, Jane."

"Just hate when you are alone, Mommy."

"Yeah. I'm okay, though, Jannie. I'm just watching my stories. You know how I love my stories. Jane, did you know Jack is the one who kidnapped—"

I interrupted her and asked about the weather. She said it was still cold and rainy and that her arthritis was acting up and wished she could take a hot bath. I began to tell her what had transpired over the past six to eight months in my career and that I was flying home to make things better for her.

She said in her sweet voice, "Jannie, you have always been a sweet daughter. I can remember walking you to kindergarten through Black Oak Park. I can see you plain as day at four years old looking up at me with your pigtails and little brown coat with fur around the collar. Do you remember that coat?"

"I think so, Mom."

"And you had your little hand inside of mine looking up at me asking me, 'Mommy, do you have my milk money?'" She laughed.

I started to cry over the phone without her knowing and said, "Mommy, now I have your milk money."

I know a lot of people don't have a strong bond with their parents, but my mother is my rock, my pillar of strength, my everything. I can't even fathom the thought of her not being here with me one day, even though I know it is the inevitable. Just thinking about it breaks my heart. If it was not for her and my dad, I would not be me. They gave me the foundation to build on, and I am so ever grateful. It's my duty and honor to take on the task of making sure she could grow old gracefully in her home. She could not believe her ears when I told her what I had been doing and how I triumphed and was never going to be in that position again. I never made her aware of my situation before because I did not want her to worry. Hell, I did not even tell my husband I was in financial disarray. I was too damn proud and knew would find a way out of my mess.

It was Wednesday evening, so I booked my flight to go home on that Monday to spend the whole week in Philly. I started putting things into play right away. The first thing I did was pay off my credit card debt, which was $50,000. Just like that, I was able to write a check out for my cards to be paid off. Then I paid $14,000 toward the mortgage, which was four months past due. I paid another $10,000 that I owed for personal shit here and there. Those three major bills were gone just like that. I cannot express to you the weight I felt lifting off my shoulders as I was paying these debts off. All I could think of was that I would never be in that position again in my life. I also decided to put my home in Philly on the market with a reputable real estate brokerage. I thought about going shopping, but I decided to wait until got back from Philly to really enjoy it.

Funny enough, this time when I boarded the plane to Philly, I felt powerful and strong. Usually, I fall right to sleep once the plane takes off, but this time I did not sleep at all. I just couldn't wait to get home and get things going for my mom. Little did she know, I had already started the process before I got there. I had four appointments set up with bathroom contractors and three appointments with new kitchen installers. She was so surprised, proud, and impressed at the same time. I loved watching her expressing what she wanted to have installed in her new bathroom so she could be safe from slips and falls.

So together we decided to do a gut remodel of the bathroom and remove the tub completely. We gave her a state-of-the-art bathroom, fully tiled and honed so she would not slip, a new oversize shower, rainforest showerheads, railings that she could hold on to while getting in and out of the shower, a large built-in shower seat, new light fixtures, toilet, and sink. It made me feel so good to see her happy.

Every so often, she would say to me, "Jannie, I can't believe you are doing this for your mom."

I would answer back, "Why not, Mommy? You did everything for me."

Then she went on to discuss the kitchen. "Put all new appliances in," I said. "Mom, tell them what you want for the back splash, flooring, and paint."

As I stood there thinking just a year ago, I had no idea how I was going to make this all happen, but now I am standing here and it is actually happening. The power of prayer, a strong work ethic, and focus made all this come to fruition.

After a full week of interviewing contractors, visiting family, and taking my mom and sisters out for dinner here and there, it was time to go back to Naples and get back to work. When I got home, I decided to sit down and share everything with my husband.

He said, "Babe, why didn't you confide in me?"

I replied, "I was just totally embarrassed and didn't want to lumber you with my problems."

I also told him I had finally decided to put the house up for sale in Philly. I had managed to hold on to it through the crash by renting it out, but for the past year, I had no tenants living there. I loved that house. It was like my Lois Lane pad in the big city. The memories will last forever.

The next morning, I slept in late because I was tired from all the traveling. When I awakened, I felt like a new person. I called my assistant, and she gave me a rundown of what was on the schedule. We had only three showings set up for the day, so I told her to take the afternoon off and I would do the showings.

It was back to the business of selling high-end real estate. Season was still going strong, and we had friends coming to visit us from Spain. Whenever I had to throw visitors in the mix, especially staying with us, it was even more draining because I had to entertain and go out to dinner, which took even more effort for me.

However, because my husband is a very social person and retired, I had to show up, if you know what I mean, and that's no fun when you're grinding, ladies.

We still had a heavy board of listings, and I was still pushing hard.

The first showing I went on, I was running fifteen minutes late because of traffic. As I pulled up, I saw the agent get out of this white four-door sedan and wave me down to let me know her customer was running late also. I thought great. Better the customer late than the agents. But I could not take my eyes off the car she got out of. It was beautiful. I got out of my little black GLK, walked right over to the car, and started asking her about the car. She said it was the new four-door Porsche Panamera. I had never seen a car so beautiful. I asked her could I sit in to see if it was roomy enough for someone tall like me, and to my surprise, it was. I never had a desire to own a Porsche, but now I did. A few hours later, she called me and said that her people were putting an offer in on my listing. I thought, *Cha-ching*. It was nothing like it. I was putting at least two to three properties under contract a month. The momentum was amazing. When I got home, I told my husband about the car, and he said that I should go for it. I didn't even know how much a Porsche cost, let alone the new four-door Panamera.

I knew Porsches were expensive, but I didn't know how expensive.

Saturday morning, we go to breakfast, and my husband said to me, "You want to stop by the Porsche dealership and check out some Porsches?"

I went, "Are you kidding me? I can't afford that. What if I don't make the money. Will you catch if I fall?"

He was like, "You can do it. Why wouldn't you make the money?"

"Because you're only as good as your last deal," I responded.

I walked into the dealership looking around, and there it was. A chocolate-black four-door Porsche Panamera with a slight sparkle in the paint. I had to take a deep breath and whispered, "Woooo, beautiful."

This baby was as aerodynamic as it gets.

I walked around the car and noticed that the ass of the car sat up and the nose slanted downward.

The interior was a sexy caramel color with a two-toned steering wheel, along with the Porsche badge smack in the middle with a little bit of red in it. The wheels were huge, and on the windshield of the car, the sticker read a cool $98,000. That's when I started laughing underneath my breath, even though I was truly already sold.

All of sudden, I turned around, and my husband was sitting down talking to the salesman. One thing I know about my husband, Mr. Frank Rostron, he is a great negotiator.

All of sudden, he asked me, "You want to take it out for a test drive, babe?"

I looked at him and said, "Babe, I can't afford this car."

"Yes, you can. You're a million-dollar real estate agent."

I looked up in the air and rolled my eyes at him. Next thing I knew, we were in the car test-driving it.

I couldn't believe I was driving this car. It felt sexy, and I felt like a million bucks driving it. *This should be mine*, I thought.

But I wanted a white one, and they did not have one, so I thought that would be my excuse not to talk about buying this car.

We went back to the dealership, and the salesman said to me, "Why don't you take it home for a few days, Jane, while I try to find you a white one?"

I said, "Oh no, it's okay. Just call us if you find one."

Of course, Frank went, "Come on, Jane. Let's take it for a few days," so I gave in.

I didn't even drive the car home. I told him to drive it. I was too nervous.

One, because it was so damn expensive, and two, I was nervous someone might run into me. The first night passed by, and I did not drive the car at all. The way my house is built, the master bedroom shower faces the driveway, so when I showered, I would just pierce outside of the window and look at the car. I could not believe I was actually thinking about buying a $100,000 car. The second day went by, and I repeated the same thing, piercing through the shutters at this beautiful monster, thinking, *I can't believe I'm going to buy this car.*

I started laughing, thinking, *I am going to buy this car because I* CAN *buy this car.*

The salesman called us that day and said he found a white one for us, but it was a turbo and $30,000 more. I said that would not work. Here it was, my chance to get out of it, and I thought there was nothing wrong with my GLK Mercedes, anyway. Then I remembered the day I went to that seminar and the speaker asked us what kind of car we drove to the event. He said he came in his Rolls-Royce Ghost. I thought, *I came in my Porsche Panamera*, and I was sold. When we drove the car back, we sat down and figured out the numbers. I handed in my little GLK and never looked back at it as I drove off the lot with a new chocolate-brown Porsche "sexy ass" Panamera. #BOSS-CEO.

The next day when I drove into work, my broker was pulling into the parking lot at the same time and grinning from ear to ear.

He was like, "That is beautiful, Ms. Bond. Is that the new Panamera?"

"Yes, it is," I replied. I asked him, "Do you think it's over the top?"

"No, Jane," he said. "You deserve it. You have worked your tail off all year. Why not buy yourself a nice car? Can I check it out?"

I said, "Go ahead."

He got in the driver's seat and drove off. I could not believe it.

Chris and I always had a great relationship from day one. He was an ex-tennis pro who got into real estate after his career was over. It was said that he was recruited by Judy Greene to come to Naples as a sitting broker of the top-grossing office in Southwest Florida, Broad Avenue South, and rightly so. He was a good guy and a very good broker, always telling jokes and always in a great mood.

He was tall and thin and wore his shirts so heavily starched. I used to make fun at him, telling him that when he took his shirt off at night, he didn't need to hang it up because it would still be standing.

He also loved music and would often come upstairs to visit me in my office to share some music he loved and would ask me if I liked it or knew of the singer. He would call me Whitney because he thought I looked like Whitney Houston. He wasn't the only one. Everyone I meet says the same thing, that I am a spitting image of

Whitney. I know I definitely can't sing like Whitney, though. LOL, I can't even sing. He made it easy to come to the office every day. Even on my bad days, Chris would make me laugh. Unfortunately, we lost him in 2018 to brain cancer.

I can very well say I loved my broker.

Chapter 6

# THE BREAKDOWN BEFORE THE BREAKTHROUGH

I felt really good. It was a new day in my life. I was debt-free and ready to kick some ass in the market. When I got upstairs to my office, my assistant told me she needed to talk to me later. I thought, *What could she want to talk about?* Everything was going well. You just never know in this business. First thing I thought, *Did I do something to offend her? Does she want a bigger percentage?* I was sitting there racking my brain and felt a little uncomfortable in my own office.

Finally, after lunch, she said, "Can I talk to you now?"

I said, "Sure, what's up?"

"I don't know how to tell you this, and I feel a little awkward because you have been so nice to me, but I think I am going to have to quit."

I was like, "What? Why?"

She said because she wanted to become a listing agent. Meaning leave me and become my competition, which is pretty much what she was telling me.

I thought, *Here we go. After all these freakin' months of training and putting systems in place, she was ready to go out on her own. Really?*

I was like, "Oh, okay."

I really didn't know how to respond at first. So I asked her what brought this on all of sudden. She blatantly told me she saw how much money I was making and felt like she was doing a lot of work but I was reaping all the benefits and that my name was on everything.

Then I thought, *But wait a minute. Is that not why I hired her? To help me grow my business and that is why my name is on everything?* She also told me that was why she wanted to work with me because I was on my way to becoming a top agent.

After she told me that, I definitely did not want her to stay.

At that moment, I felt defeated, and here it was, I thought I was having a great day. New attitude, new Porsche Panamera, money in the bank, and now this! There will always be a monkey wrench thrown into the ring. You just better be prepared to catch it or fucking duck. Here it is, I had put all my trust into this girl, and now she was letting me down by telling me she was leaving.

Then she continued on by saying that she would stay with me until the season was over and after that, she was moving on. I was thinking, *The hell you will.*

*Now, do I keep her on until season is over because I need the help, or do I just let her go now?* Two seconds later, that option went right out the window.

Letting her go now was the best thing for me. I knew I could handle things on my own because I did it before having an assistant. Plus, I taught her everything she knew. This was a huge lesson learned and prepared me for what was to come. That was the furthest thing from my mind today, her telling me she wanted to go out on her own.

A lot of agents think they can do what top agents can do until they actually get out there. It took me four years before the lightbulb even came on just to understand that I needed a coach. It also takes years to learn how to deal with people of a certain caliber and stature in life. Sometimes it can be a difficult task for young agents to even get work with this type of customer.

A conservative businessman is going to be a little apprehensive about having a young agent purchase a five-million-dollar home for his family—unless he feels secure with their business acumen as a sales agent, and rightly so. It not only takes an agent having knowledge of their market; it takes negotiation skills and having the right resources in place to shepherd the transaction through to the finish line. The number one question agents should ask themselves upon taking clients is, *How can add value to this customer's experience with me?*

When you are a listing agent, it's not just about taking on a listing. You have to be able to keep those listings on the market with marketing and advertising dollars. I remember asking one agent why didn't she become a listing agent, and she simply told me she could not afford to become a listing agent. That was another thing they didn't teach you in real estate school—that you need actual marketing dollars to market a customer's listings.

When we finished out the day, I turned to her and said, "I have come to a decision that it would be best that you left now as opposed to leaving at the end of the season."

She looked at me like a deer in headlights. I was sure she was a little taken aback by my decision.

However, what she did not understand was that she became my competition as soon as she shared with me that she wanted to go out on her own. Therefore, it was time for her to get up out of my office and my face.

When I got home, I told Frank what had happened, and he said I would just have to buckle down a little more.

That same evening, our friends arrived from Spain to visit us. I noticed right away that one of them had a nasty cough, and I thought, *Oh hell no, he sounds god-awful terrible. I hope I don't get sick, man.*

All night while entertaining our guests, I thought about what had just happened at work with my employee. And you know what I thought? *The hell with that. I started out on my own, and I will be just fine, because no one is going to stop my goals to create the life I want but me.*

Whenever you're trying to achieve something great, the devil is always on his job, but not on my watch! I went to bed that night pumped and ready for the next day. I had customers that depended on me to get the damn job done, and that was to sell their home. When I got in the next morning, my phone did not stop ringing. I set up four showings for the day and decided to prospect for a couple of hours until it was time for the first showing. I glanced up at the wall and saw that there were only eight listings left. I started to feel a little anxious, thinking I needed more listings to sell because keeping the pipeline full was the goal. If you don't have listings, then you don't have anything to sell, and I definitely did not want to go back down that road. Before leaving out, I stopped by my broker's office to share with him that I lost my assistant. He shared with me that the next person I hire, I should make sure they definitely do not want to sell real estate because it never works out, and they always end up leaving anyway.

I just shook my head, smiled, and said, "Got it," and walked out.

After the first two showings, I started to feel a little queasy, but I continued to work, driving to the next showing, which was in Bonita Springs, about thirty minutes north of Naples. When I arrived, to my surprise, I knew the buyer from a couple of years ago. I had taken him out, but he was not ready to buy at that time, and I don't think he was ready to buy today either. All I could think was that he was probably wasting this poor agent's time as he did mine back then. I remembered him running me around like crazy, putting offers in and never accepting counter from the seller. After the third or fourth time, I just never took him out again and dodged his calls. By the time I got to the last showing, I felt exhausted, so I opened up the property and went back to my car to wait for the agent. After sitting there for twenty minutes, I decided to call the agent.

She told me that they had driven by the property earlier and the buyer decided not to see the property. So I asked her why did she not give me a call and that I had been sitting there waiting for her for the past twenty minutes.

She simply said, "I'm sorry. I totally forgot."

I told her thank you and hung up. I'm sure she knew I was pretty unhappy with her.

Now agents, how the hell do you forget to call someone you know is going to be there waiting for you? That is just pure rudeness and unprofessional to do to a fellow agent. Rule number one: never leave another agent hanging in the wind. Now not only am I feeling queasy, I have a very bad headache too, so I set out to go home. All the way home, I was thinking, *Boy oh boy, these are not symptoms of being exhausted. These are symptoms of a cold.*

I got home, and Frank took one look at me and said, "Baby, you look like hell. Are you feeling well?"

"No," I told him, "and I'm going right to bed."

I took a shower and got in bed and started to shiver. Needless to say, I had come down with the flu just that quick. The next day, I couldn't even get out of bed, and of course, our guests left and I got right down for the count. I was thinking, *This cannot be happening. I don't have anyone to pick up the slack for my customers. No one to do showings or an open house. I am so fucked and sick as a dog.* My business came to a complete halt for the next nine days straight.

I couldn't eat, I couldn't sleep, and I was so stuffed up in the night. I lay awake all night with aches and pains, and it was almost morning when I could finally get some rest. My head was killing me because the cold was in my head and chest. At this point, I was suffering from sleep deprivation and constant nausea. It felt like nothing was making me feel better. So Frank took me to the doctor, and the doctor diagnosed me with influenza B, one of the worst strains of flu going around.

The doctor prescribed me Tamiflu, an antiviral drug that I took for four days, and finally, I started to feel better. My fever broke, and the aches and pains went away. All I can say is that it felt like I was in complete hell for the past nine days. After coming back from the dead, I needed another five days before I could actually go back to work.

You talk about the breakdown before the breakthrough. Well, I definitely went through the breakdown. Not only did I get sick from the flu, I also suffered from chronic fatigue. I was in bad shape for two weeks. I had not showed any of my properties for the past two weeks, and I had to answer to a couple of my customers who were upset that their property had not sold as of yet. We all know this is a numbers game, and not all properties are going to sell for whatever reason. I still had seven properties that had not moved when I came back from being sick, but the truth of the matter was, I really did not get any calls on them while I was sick. Now season was coming to a close, and I ended up selling one last listing. For the others, I still had them under contract for six months, so I just kept showing them.

I decided to take it a little easy after the season and regroup. I had worked harder than I had ever worked before in my life, and it paid off. I was able to do everything I had set out to do for my mom and more. I was not worried about being in debt anymore because I was completely debt-free, and it felt good to finally be able to breathe without the stress and worry of what was coming next from my past problems.

Two months had passed by, and the season was completely over. All the tourists had left, and the streets and beaches were empty again. This was when Naples and real estate usually flatline and we get our city back. I started hitting the phones again, but nothing was happening because of the mind-set of Neapolitans and Naples being a second-home market. The primary homeowners did not want to put their homes on the market, and the second homeowners were not here. When you would reach out to them up north, they felt there was no need at this time because there were no buyers in the market, which was the truth.

But I knew I had to continue to keep some sort of momentum up to keep making money. Because even though I was not worried anymore and out of debt, I had upped my game with a new Porsche Panamera and new wardrobe. This was when the lightbulb went off and I got the idea to expand my business by going over to the other coast.

Why not? It was a two-and-a-half-hour drive back and forth, and there was a Sotheby's office in South Beach. So I sat down with Frank and shared with him what my plan was. Of course, he was not too happy about it, but it just did not matter because when I set my mind on doing something, there is pretty much no turning me back.

The next day, I went in the office and discussed it with my broker, and he shared with me that he thought it was going to be difficult to go back and forth every day. But I needed to at least go and try because that is just who I am as a person. I have to keep moving the goal post.

The next day, I started making phone calls and setting up appointments to see the managing broker with One Sotheby's in Miami for the following week. I knew I would not have a problem getting into the office because my numbers were good, and I had done really well this past season. As we know, it is all about the numbers, your gross commission income (GCI). I went over to Miami, and it was everything I expected it to be—diversified, exciting, and lots of energy.

I met with the managing broker, and I was told it was not a problem for me to join the Miami office and that I could start when I was ready. I was ecstatic because I was about to break into another market and expand my business.

I went back and forth for a couple of weeks, just to kind of get the lay of the land and network with some of the agents while they were getting my paperwork together. But there was only one problem. I had to leave my Naples office because Sotheby's was a franchise, and it was a different business even though it carried the brand's name. Wow, that hit me like a lightning bolt. Little did I know that Sotheby's was a franchise. I thought it was owned by one company. And as an agent, you can only hang your license with one company in any state. It is illegal to hang it with two different companies in any one state. Talk about a monkey wrench thrown in the mix. This was a huge problem for me. All my business was in Naples, and it would be like starting all over again, and that was not what I had in mind. I just simply wanted to expand my business.

Now, I was faced with another decision that I was not willing to make at this time, so I decided to rethink my plan. While traveling back and forth to the Miami office, I had met a really nice agent. I decided to call her and tell her about my dilemma, and just like that, she and I came up with a solution. We decided to join forces where she would list any properties I would get, and we would do a 65/35 split with a sliding scale depending on price and time.

It was great. I was able to get the MLS and a second mojo account to call on expireds. I started generating new leads almost immediately.

While Naples had flatlined, Miami was just revving up for their season.

I would get in my car at 6:30 a.m. and be in Miami Beach by 9:00 a.m., providing the traffic was good. But if I ran into traffic, it became hellish. People in Miami drove like maniacs compared to Naples. But I didn't care. I still got up every morning and drove over to learn as much as I could. I started seeing the differences in the companies as I began to go on presentations with the tools that were available to me.

I also did not know we had to pay a monthly fee just to walk through the door and say we belonged to One Sotheby's. And to make matters even worse, there was no place to sit or store your paperwork. As an agent, the reason you choose a brokerage to hang your license with is because your brokerage is supposed to provide you with the systems and tools for you to do your job properly, and hopefully, you become successful at it. Then I was told after a certain amount of copies, I had to pay. I thought, *Why are they nickel and diming their agents?* We are the ones out here on the grind with our ears to the ground, bringing in the bacon, and we still have to give them somewhat a major cut of our money. *Boy oh boy*, I thought, *I have it made in Naples with Premier Sotheby's.* But I was desperate for something new and exciting, and I wanted to expand my business so badly. So I kept going back and forth every week. After six months, I realized this was much harder than I thought. Even though the process was the same as far as prospecting, the drive was just so grueling. If I did not leave the beach by three thirty, I could not leave until after seven, or I would be stuck in bumper-to-bumper traffic for two hours just to get off the beach. It was already pretty much a five-hour drive, and this would turn it into a six-hour drive. Not only that, it started to wreak havoc on my marriage.

My husband hated that I would leave out very early in the morning and get home sometimes at ten o'clock at night, or much later if there was an event that I attended. Even more, I had to drive alone across Alligator Alley, a very dark ninety-mile stretch on I-75 that lots of people have been known to fall asleep and crash. And the reason it's called Alligator Alley is because on both sides of the road behind the fence, there are swamps with lots of alligators living in them. But I did not want to give it up because I had just started getting some traction and I liked the energy of it all. Naples was so sleepy with no diversity, and sometimes, it was just so exhausting. What my husband did not understand was that not only did I need it to expand my business, I needed it for my soul and spirit culturally, and that was very hard to explain to him when I had found success in Naples.

My new Miami associate was lovely, poised, and articulate, and we got along well. Unfortunately, for the time I had spent going back and forth, we were not able to secure a deal. While I was over there, I had also started to look into other brokerage houses like Douglas Elliman, Compass, and Coldwell Banker and introducing myself to the brokers. Interesting enough, when I met with the DE broker, we got along really well. DE is a NYC brokerage house known for its well-heeled, well-dressed glossy agents who take pride in dressing well and *showing up for the part*, as we say in real estate. They were also known for their agents being on the hot new Bravo network show, *Million-Dollar Listing NYC, LA, and Miami*. The agents were good-looking, dressed impeccably well, making million-dollar deals happen on a daily basis, and they made it look easy.

I can very well say that the shows changed the whole landscape in which we look at real estate as an industry. It is not your momma's business anymore. It is high finance, beautiful people, and lots of money to be made.

Chapter 7

# NETWORKING IS KEY

DE had exploded on the seen in Miami a few years ago, at the helm of Jay, who was well-known and well liked. He came from the title business end of real estate. He also looked the part, was well connected, and was a very good talker. Jay liked the fact that I was in Naples and said that they were exploring the thought of opening up an office there because of the amount of high-end real estate and wealth that was in Naples. I found this very interesting also because the thought process immediately was that I could open up their office. I had a lot to offer as far as knowing the Naples market and could help them recruit good, solid agents. I found this to be very exciting. Over the next few months, Jay stayed in touch with me every now and then.

I also interviewed with the new startup real estate company Compass, in which I was very impressed.

Compass had this new, clean, fresh, and contemporary feel to their marketing. Their systems and tools, coupled with technology, was hot, which made them a very strong candidate to be considered in the future.

All summer long as I was going back and forth over to the other coast, I was still prospecting in Naples and had set my sights on this one particular listing. It was on Marco Island, but well worth the thirty-minute drive to the island. Hell, I even drove to Sanibel at one time and purchased a million-dollar house for a referral customer. It actually was one of the easy sales I had. This particular listing had been off and on the market for $12–10 million. I knew if I could land that listing, it would change the game for me. I had already weathered the storm of losing my assistant in the middle of season, falling sick with a virus, and dealing with chronic fatigue.

Nevertheless, I still came out on top as a rising star.

However, I knew I had to do it all over again and more to solidify the title of becoming a top, well-respected agent in my market. I now understood what consistency, follow-up, and concierge service was and what was expected from me as a high-end agent. But I had to prove myself all over again by landing more listings than I had before at a higher price point. We all know in this business that you are only as good as your last sale. It was mid-August, and I had been working like crazy with the driving back and forth and prospecting every day. I realized it was time to look for another assistant/buyer's agent to handle transactions and customers while I was traveling back and forth.

I remembered that I had met this lovely, expressive young man at a videotaping of a show for realtors in Naples. His name was Nick Imperato, and I loved his energy. Of course, he was from up north, in DC.

I believe I looked all over for his card and called him the next day and asked if we could meet for lunch, and he agreed. We met at Campiello's, an open-air bar and restaurant, somewhat of a scene in Naples. We laughed and talked for about two hours. He was just what I was looking for in an assistant. Smart, quick, funny, and lovely to be around.

I asked him to come work with me at Sotheby's as my assistant and buyer's agent. He said yes. We shook and I told him to come by the office the next day so we could map out the particulars and so he could also meet my broker, Chris.

After Nick met with Chris, Chris came up to my office and solidified what I had already known—that I picked a winner and a smart cookie and that he was giving him a chance with a decent split. This made our negotiations make complete sense with bringing him on. Nick expressed how excited he was to have this opportunity.

He recognized that being able to come on board with Sotheby's as a young agent and work alongside me was huge.

His timing could not have been more perfect. It seemed as though everyone liked him right away. He was young, cute, and a pleasure to be around.

We were always laughing, and funny enough, we actually cried some days. I found that my clients fell in love with him also, despite his youth. Nick could carry a conversation; he was very well read and had graduated cum laude from George Mason University.

He was punctual and understood the business and was really thorough when it came to using the MLS and daily statistics.

It was great once Nick and I got into a rhythm, and the work-flow was good.

September rolled around, and my husband decided it was time we took a break and visited Europe before season started up again. I was a little freaked out about leaving Naples at first, but I decided he was right. We needed a much long-awaited vacation from it all, and I had Nick who was very capable of handling things while I was gone.

Besides, I had not spent any quality time with my husband in a while. So we booked our trip and packed up, and off to Europe we went.

We visited England, Majorca, Barcelona, Rome, and Venice. It was amazing. We got to see family in England and quite a few friends. It was always a whirlwind in England. Dinner every night and lunch every day with at least ten people. England is Frank's home, and he is very well-known there, so we are always completely booked before we hit the ground.

This trip was going to be a little different this time around because had set out to visit a Sotheby's office in every country to network and create relationships—something I had never thought about doing before. Being with an internationally known company like Sotheby's, you were able to forge relationships around the world.

Especially in London, which was our first stop. I went into the Sotheby's office in London a couple of blocks away from the auction house, and the office was in complete chaos because they were in the middle of moving. However, I did get to meet a couple of young realtors who were excited to meet me and wanted to stay in touch and build a relationship in the future. Then I went down to the auction house and gallery. It was exquisite with incredible art pieces, which completely moved me.

I have to say, I felt very proud at that moment to belong to such a prestigious establishment. From England, we traveled to Rome and Venice.

Rome and Venice were so special to visit because it was the first time my husband had ever visited either. I, on the other hand, had visited Rome many, many times and also lived in Venice for a while as a young flight attendant. So I got to revisit my old stomping grounds in Venice and see old friends. We stayed at the beautiful world-famous Danieli Hotel. The Danieli is one of the oldest and traditional venetian hotels in Venice, located right off San Marco Square and steps away from the famous Harry's Bar. This was right up my husband's alley. He loves when we get dressed up and go out to dinner, but he likes to make an evening out of it by going out for cocktails first. Well, Italy lends to this completely. It's romantic and fashionable. So of course, we dressed up every night for dinner. I must admit, I like looking good when I go out too, and I had made quite a bit money this year. So for the first time in a long time, I could shop as much as I wanted to without asking my husband. That is the beauty of selling million-dollar properties.

I introduced Frank to some great friends, including one really good friend, Renato Salmaso, who owns the restaurant Da Raffaela. If you ever get the opportunity to visit Venice, his restaurant is a must, and please mention my name. LOL. The food is amazing, and he is from one of the first families of Venice.

His family also owns Ala Hotel and the romantic Pensione Accademia Hotel, which is very beautiful and well maintained. I feel very grateful and fortunate to have kept such a long and wonderful friendship going for so many years and that we could introduce our husbands and wives to each other. We had a great night of reminiscing about old times and old friends. Friendships are a wonderful thing, especially a friendship of twenty-five years. That evening, we also said our long goodbyes.

The next day, I hit the ground visiting Sotheby's Venice, which was a small but beautiful office in a lovely building. Unfortunately, the manager was not in, so I just left my card, and surprisingly, he e-mailed me when I got back to America. The next day, we traveled over to the beautiful Cipriani Hotel for lunch and the only hotel that had a swimming pool at that time in Venice, if you can imagine. What a beautiful place to sit out and have lunch.

Later that day, we packed up, and off to Rome we went. We get to our hotel in Rome, the St. Regis Grand Palais, formerly known as the Grand Hotel. It is absolutely beautiful, flowers everywhere. Before we left Venice, we asked Renato and his wife to recommend a few restaurants to go to while in Rome, being as though they were restaurant owners. Once we arrived at the hotel, we asked the concierge which restaurant was the best to have dinner at. The concierge said that Antica Pesa, by far, was the best restaurant, so we made reservations for that evening.

Once I unpacked and relaxed for an hour or so, I went out to find the Rome's Sotheby's to meet an agent, Diletta Giorgolo S., whom I had researched.

She represented some of the most expensive real estate in all of Italy. Her father was a former ambassador. Unfortunately for me, she was in Tuscany. Being the networker I am, I got her on the phone, and she said she was sad that she missed me and that I should stay in touch and let her know of my plans to come back to Rome in the future.

She also e-mailed me the same day and mentioned a couple of colleagues she was very friendly with from One Sotheby's.

That evening, we traveled to Trastevere, a neighborhood in Rome, to eat at Antica Pesa. I learned later on that Antica Pesa stood for antique scales. Since the seventeenth century, villagers in Vatican City used scales to portion food brought in from local farmers to give to the less fortunate.

In 1922, the Panella family opened a restaurant in the nearby Roman neighborhood, Trastevere, and named it Antica Pesa, in support of the generosity of their fellow countrymen.

OMG, the food was beyond crazy good, and it was a very swanky place.

We noticed right away from walking into the place that all of Hollywood came to this place. The wall was full of pictures of the owners and every big-named star in America.

Leave it to us to choose the one restaurant that all of Hollywood frequents in Rome. We also found out that there is one in America, and in of all places, Williamsburg, Brooklyn. We will definitely be visiting that one too. Needless to say, we had a great night. And to top it off, we decided to have a nightcap at our beautiful hotel bar.

While we sat there having a nightcap, this couple came in and sat down next to us. We began to chat, and they asked us if we had dinner at Antica Pesa this evening. We said yes. Ironically, they had dinner there too. We all agreed how great the restaurant and the food was.

We then asked what part of America they were from, and to our surprise, they said Orlando, Florida. We started laughing and told them we were from Naples, which is only three hours away. We carried on drinking and getting to know one another. I thought she was funny and beautiful, and Frankie seemed to like them too. It seemed like we hit it off as couples. We decided to have dinner the next evening with our new friends Jack and Debbie Liberti at another restaurant that was recommended to the both of us. We finished our drinks and headed to the elevators laughing our heads off.

When we hit our floor button, funny enough, they were on the same floor as we were and not only the same floor, but they were staying right next door to us. Now we were laughing really loud, and someone screamed, "Shut up and go to bed!" from their hotel room.

At that moment, Frank had the bright idea to bang on that person's door and tell them to shut up. You should have seen all of us scramble to get in our rooms laughing our heads off. I almost peed my pants. We were acting like college kids with the Libertis. It was a lot of fun.

*What a great way to enjoy Rome*, I thought, *with another crazy couple.*

The next day, we went to the Vatican City, and there were about two thousand people waiting in line to go in.

I looked at Frank and said, "Come on, I see our friends. They're up there in front. I can't believe they did not wait for us!"

Frank was looking at me like I was crazy because I was talking to myself and we were not with any friends. He went, "What I said. Just come on," as people started to look at us.

I just kept waving and saying, "Hey, wait for us." We made our way all the way up to the front of the line and just stood there, and it just so happened, a girl turned around and started talking to me, and I said, "I can't believe our friends went in without us."

She was American. She said, "What? Girl, that's terrible."

I said, "Right."

Frank was totally embarrassed. I asked her where was she from, and she said she was from Philly. I told her I was from Philly too. "Isn't that cool?"

She replied, "Yes."

We high-fived each other and continued walking into the Vatican together.

And just like that, we were inside.

*Ha!* Frank was like, "What a little jibber you are."

He could not believe it. Just ten minutes ago, we were at the back of the line behind two thousand people, and now we were standing inside looking at the Sistine Chapel. I was happy because he wanted to turn around and leave, and I knew he really was looking forward to going inside the Vatican. Who wouldn't? The biggest mistake we made was to go all the way to the top of the Vatican. I mean up to the very top. It was the scariest thing ever. Once I was almost up to the top, I realized this was a bad idea when I saw people on the way up that could not make it. They were sitting on the staircase or in little alcoves. I thought, *What the hell are we doing?* Once we got to a certain point, there was no turning back.

You could not turn around because the staircase was so narrow you could not get past people coming up behind you. All I could think of was what idiots we were and that we could die up here. I started praying, saying, *God, if you let me get back down safely, I will never do anything this stupid again.* I was so relieved to get back on the ground I did not know what to do but thank God. I don't think we will ever want to see anything that bad ever again.

At dinner that night, I shared with Jack and Debbie what had happened, and we had a good laugh. But I warned them not to go up to the top and that it would be foolish. While we were at dinner, I got a phone call from America, and lo and behold, it was Jay from Douglas Elliman asking me if I was in town and that he had a possible eight-million-dollar listing for me in Naples. I can't believe my ears and my phone bill after the call. I got off the phone and shared the news with Frank and the Libertis. Like I always say, the power of getting out and networking always pays off at some point in time. I truly can say throughout my career, networking has been the biggest ROI for me. I am so excited because I only met him once, and for him to feel as though I could handle an eight-million-dollar listing was huge in my head.

I shared with him that I was in Rome. How cool was that? That I was in Rome taking a call for an eight-million-dollar referral. This would be my biggest listing, if I got it. No, *when* I got it, because he was seeking me out while I was in Rome hanging out and chillin'. LOL. I told him that I would reach out to him as soon as I got back to the states. That was an amazing night, and the next day, I could not stop thinking about the call. We had breakfast with Jack and Debbie, exchanged info, and said our goodbyes because we were leaving that day to fly to Mallorca, then to Barcelona. Jack and Debbie were staying in Italy a little longer. This was also a very weird time to be in Europe because it was during the time of the Europe Migrant Crisis. Europe was facing a populist uprising, and every TV channel was covering it. I have to say, I felt like if anything broke out, we could go to a Sotheby's office and find refuge with someone there because there was an office everywhere we went. I was connecting with everyone, every time we would land in Europe. It was like a safe haven. The news can scare the living daylights out of you if you let it.

We arrived in Mallorca that afternoon, and it was absolutely beautiful. I immediately fell in love with it. We stayed at this cool hotel that was African inspired. The Hotel Lindner in Bendinat, I loved it! I believe it was German owned. It was time to relax. We had been running all around Italy seeing the sights because it was Frankie's first time there.

The hotel had a great pool area where you could sit, have lunch, and just chill. We met up with some friends there from Denmark, Germany, and England. This was Frankie's old stomping grounds. He actually owned a house there for over twenty some odd years.

A lot of friends had flown into Mallorca to attend a party that he put together of at least two hundred people. We went into Palma and then drove to Port Andratx to the Sotheby's office, where I met with Monika Baier, who was just so amazing and open to whatever I had to bring to the table. I loved that she was a real networker too. I could have sat with her all day talking about business.

Mallorca reminded me of Venice with its medieval feel. Its little streets that twist and turn at every corner, almost never ending, magical too! Little quaint coffee and sandwich shops everywhere with fashionable boutiques along the way. The people were alive and very friendly. We had to hurry back to the hotel to get ready for the party. I was so tired from the day and could not stop thinking about that phone call from America. *An eight-million-dollar listing. Wow!* Even though I was having a great time, all I could think about was getting back home to see how the referral was going to play itself out. The party was fun. Friends came from all over Europe to come to the party.

Frank got to see all his old friends, and he seemed very happy to see them. They played old videos, sang, and danced the night away. I was really happy to see Frank have fun. We all met at the beach the next day for brunch and continued to party. So much for relaxing. We laughed all day. I can't remember laughing so much until my mouth was hurting. I was so tired when we got back to the hotel. I just lay out by the pool and fell asleep until it was time to go out to dinner. Going out at night in Mallorca was like being in a movie scene.

Our last night we went to a restaurant called Mason Ca'n Pedro, located in the hills of Mallorca, outside of the city of Palma. I love the Gypsy Kings, but that evening they had a Spanish Mariachi band there that was pretty cool, dressed in all the garb, wearing big sombreros and playing acoustic guitars. It was really a lot fun; they took lots of pictures of me dancing and singing in a sombrero.

Goodbye, Mallorca. Hello, Barcelona! My first time ever in Barcelona, and wow! The architecture was so mysterious and beautiful at the same time.

Our hotel, Hotel Claris, was different too. The thing that comes to mind every time I say Claris is Hannibal Lecter from *Silence of the Lambs*.

Jody Foster's name was Claris. Nothing to do with the hotel, but that is what comes to my morbid mind. I guess because I am a lover of scary movies. Gaudi's work was everywhere and really different. It looked like the buildings were wearing masks. *A strange twist to modernism*, I thought, especially Park Güell.

There were tapas restaurants everywhere with delicious small bites of succulent garlic shrimp, sliced calamari, hot tomato, and brisket. Just walking around this beautiful city of culture, style, and harmony, I found Barcelona to be captivating and fascinating because of its sophistication and the way it catered to the blending of cultures.

The whole time I walked around looking for the Sotheby's office, I found myself looking up and stopping every few feet to take in the aesthetics of the mix of tradition and modernism of architecture.

Finally, I found the office tucked away upstairs in this building, which was also museum. I met one agent there, and he was nice and sat with me talking about the difference between the American and European real estate markets. He expressed that he always wanted to live in America and sell real estate. Funny, because I told him if I had discovered Barcelona when I was a flight attendant, I would have spent quite some time visiting back and forth. We both had a good laugh and said our goodbyes before parting ways. As I walked back to the hotel, stumbled onto the Madison Avenue of Barcelona. Talk about fabulous fashions—everything was very sexy and cutting-edge.

When I arrived back at the hotel, I was so excited because I had accomplished just what I had set out to do. That was to network all through Europe, meeting and connecting with agents. It was a good feeling. That night, I was going to one of the best restaurants in Barcelona to close out our European vacation. We went to Nuba Lounge in the uptown part of Barcelona.

Unfortunately, we got there a little earlier than we should have for dinner, but the food was great, and the beautiful people were coming as we were about to leave. We decided to stay a little longer to people watch by having a couple of after-dinner cocktails. But after a while, we were wiped out and ready for bed. The next day, we packed up early and went out to lunch before leaving to the airport. What a trip.

Three and half weeks of traveling, eating, drinking, and gaining weight.

Ugh, I can very well say I was done and ready to be back home. Up, up, and away, we went back to America.

By the time we got home, it was about ten in the evening. Being the anal person that I am, I needed to unpack and put all the dirty clothes in the washer before going to bed. As soon as I got up the next morning and got dressed, I called Jay of Douglas Elliman and told him I was back in the States.

He put things right into motion, connecting me with the agent who had the referral for the eight-million-dollar listing. However, this property was on Marco Island, forty minutes from Naples and across the bridge. What a coincidence that it was in the same building as the ten-million-dollar listing I had set my sights on, and both were penthouses. One was sixteen thousand square feet, and the other was over nine thousand square feet. Can you say top agent?

I call Nick to let him know I was back in the States and to share with him the phone call I received. I told Nick we had to do our research on the New York agent that had the referral before speaking with her. She turned out to be a very accomplished and well-known agent in NYC. When I spoke with her, we discussed the lifestyle of the potential referral and what they were trying to accomplish by selling this penthouse. She also shared with me that the husband was very analytical and the family had been in the commercial airline industry and divesting some of their assets. By gathering this information, I knew the level of customer I was dealing with, and I was able to better prepare for the presentation.

# Chapter 8

......................................

# IT'S SHOWTIME

A few days later, I received a call from the seller, and we set up the appointment for the very next day. All that night, I prepared for the presentation for him and his wife. Before leaving out that morning, I called Nick to discuss my game plan, just for reassurance.

When I arrived at the Belize building late that morning, I felt confident and pretty calm. It kind of weirded me out, and then I realized it was the calmness of knowing my shit and being ready for the kill.

The husband met me in the lobby of the building and seemed a little surprised that I was Jane Bond, because he said to me, "So you're Jane Bond."

I guess he did not expect a six feet tall black woman. But he was really friendly. I take a quick look around the building and realized it was a WCI building. Twenty-six stories high, situated directly on the beach. Ornate as hell, filled with brass railings everywhere and large fish tanks, a theatre room, clubroom, lobby bar, guest rooms for overflow of guest, and a beautiful pool that lay alongside the building overlooking the Gulf of Mexico.

The building was also on the largest barrier reef of the ten thousand islands on Marco, which lends to a spectacular view from any of the penthouses.

As we rode up in the elevator, we exchanged niceties. He asked me how was the high-end market doing, which is a totally typical question one would ask. Then the elevator doors opened to the penthouse, and my initial thoughts were, *Drab and dark*. But it was partially decorator ready, nine thousand square feet with amazing views surrounded by the ten thousand islands and sitting on the largest barrier reefs on the Gulf of Mexico. Not a bad sell.

It had a lot of potential to be absolutely fabulous if you want to live on Marco Island, where it is quiet, and if you're a boat enthusiast. If this checks all your boxes, then this is the perfect place. I have to say, when you come over the bridge into Marco, there is a sense of relief. Somehow, I always manage to take a deep breath. Unfortunately, there is really nothing exciting on Marco Island to do, and there is only one way in and one way out.

This penthouse was in the best building, with the best amenities, and with low carrying cost. There was definitely value in it for the next buyer at the right price. As we flowed through the penthouse, we spoke about how we could start the marketing wheel for the property, sharing plenty of conversation about resources and what our initial plan could look like. I saw that all the bathrooms in the penthouse were modernized but were still dated. The master suite needed a complete overhaul, along with the bathroom. This looked more like a $6.5-million listing with a negotiating window of $1.5 million at time of market. Yes, the views were million-dollar views, but how do I justify the other $5 million? We take the elevator to another floor in the building, and to my surprise, they lived in the building in another penthouse. Today, penthouses are not always defined by being on the top floor. They are sometimes defined by the square footage.

I was directed into a room of the penthouse to sit and wait for his wife to come in and join us. His wife comes in and immediately starts sizing me up after we exchange hellos. Ladies, now you know what I'm talking about. The four-finger handshake, like they barely want to touch you, the eyeballing you up and down, the not-so-nice stare with the forefinger above the top lip rubbing it across the nostrils, as if something smells, the thumb under the chin, and the quiet treatment, pretty much the whole time you're speaking.

This could be quite intimidating to some agents, but I did not pay any attention to that shit. Because like I said, I knew my shit and was ready for any questions they threw at me. She finally broke her silence by asking me how I was going to market the empty raw space.

I kindly started out the conversation with, "The only way I believe we would get people interested is to paint the picture for them because most people cannot visualize."

She nodded as to give me permission to continue, so I did.

"Especially a property of this size, but if we lighten up the paint color throughout the common areas, stage the bedrooms and bathrooms properly, and have virtual renderings of the home online, this could garner some interest. We also could put a large flat screen in the property and have a video of the virtual renderings on loop mode, so when it's shown to potential buyers, they could envision what the property could look like."

At that moment, the wife perked up and asked, "And what would you suggest we put the property on the market for?"

I firmly said, "Six point five million."

"Oh, no," she said.

"We will not sell it for less than 7 million." So I shared with them the state of the luxury market, the comps, and also the fact that the property was decorator ready and dated, irrespective of the square footage and view.

Also, the fact that they would need some room for negotiating and the numbers don't lie.

"Everything is public record today. Customers are going to look at time held by seller, time spent on the market, and if the customer has done any upgrades to warrant the price, so we have to take all of these things into consideration," I said. Then I started talking about how beautiful, bright, and inviting their penthouse was when you stepped off the elevator. You immediately wanted to see more.

Finally, I get a smile from the wife and she said, "Yes, I did the work in here myself."

I was like, "You did an outstanding job from the little bit of the condo I have seen. It has a sort of Parisian flair. I used to live in Paris, and it reminds me of some of the homes I was in."

"Oh, you lived in Paris?" she asked.

"Yes, and also Venice for about thirteen months."

"So where do you summer?" she asked.

That came out of nowhere. I thought, *Where do I summer? LOL.*
The first thing came to mind was, *Right here in Naples. It's ninety-nine damn degrees pretty much all year round.* I had never been asked a question like this before, so I simply said, "When it gets too hot here, my husband and I travel to Napa. However, we travel to a lot of places like England, Dubai, and South Africa. We travel to England a lot because he is English."

She all of sudden stood up and said, "Would you like to see the rest of the house?"

I thought, *Well, damn, I must have impressed her.* She started asking me questions about Abu Dhabi, probably to see if I actually had gone there. These questions were very specific to an area in Abu Dhabi that you would more than likely only know about the area unless you had been there.

I thought that was pretty funny. Wealthy people can be very interesting people. They love it if you play in their sandbox of travel, money, and success. Success begets success. I was told a long time ago, *"Show up, look good, and keep your mouth shut if you don't know."*

Listening is key in most situations, and you might just learn something. After the tour of their amazing private penthouse, we sat back down in the parlor. They began to share with me that they liked my marketing plan of action and that I seemed very knowledgeable of the high-end market.

I gave them my prelisting package and said, "Thank you for having me over, and I look forward to hearing from you."

I left the penthouse still feeling very confident, even though they did not sign the contract. I called Nick and told him all the tee, and we just kee-keed while I drove back to the office.

The next day, the husband called me, and I just knew I had the listing, but he just wanted to ask me a few more questions and told me he was entertaining another agent at another brokerage. In my mind, I was like, *Okayyy.* So pried a little more, and once he shared the info, I told him that we are an international company with a network of agents around the world that could cater to a listing of this magnitude and that I would share his listing throughout that network. He simply thanked me and told me he would call me back, one way or another. That was when I got a little nervous and started thinking about the ten-million-dollar listing and that maybe I was just too self-assured and cocky, and now I was not going to get the listing. I started to feel a little depressed, thinking I screwed up.

As the day went on, I kept looking at my phone, hoping that he called me back. I got home from the day, and I was pulling into my garage, still thinking how stupid I was for acting that way. My phone rang, and it was him, the seller, letting me know that I got the freaking listing and that they wanted to put the property on the market for—as I held my breath—$7 million.

I had the biggest sigh of relief. It's one thing to get the listing. It's another to sell it. And it's even harder trying to sell a grossly overpriced listing.

Nick Imperato

Chapter 9

........................................

# THE MARKETING GAME

I was so excited I could hardly contain myself over the phone. I told him was going to get right on it. He asked that I get in touch with their interior designer to discuss the painting as soon as possible. I was in top-agent heaven. I called Nick and told him the news that we got the listing, and he could not believe it.

Just putting this listing on my books made me look great. I was moving on up to the eastside, literally, to the penthouse in the sky!

LOL. This was a game changer for my price point.

Now, I was equipped to go after the mother of all mothers: the $10-million penthouse. I decided to rewrite my lead letter to specifically go after this listing. I had called the prospect several times, and he told me he was not interested and that all of us agents said the same thing and made the same empty promises before hanging up on me. But that did not discourage me. I was taught to keep following up because customers that did not sell their property the first time around, or even in this case, the second time around, are going through a frustrated period and just need a little time to get through it.

So I waited a couple of weeks, which gave me time to get the $7-million penthouse. By doing a little research, I was able to find an up-north address, phone number, and the customer's identity. Man, don't ever underestimate the power of the Internet's information bank. I found out what he did for a living and how he became successful. That a very well-known park was named after him and he loved driven people. I called the number and spoke with a really nice older lady. I told her that I was a realtor and I was looking to send him a letter.

"Would he receive it if I sent it to this address?" I asked.

She said of course and that she would get it delivered to him. When I hung up with her, I felt really good about what I had accomplished. Just by going that extra mile, I was able to get in touch with a nice lady who was going to get the letter to him. A couple of weeks passed by, and I got an unexpected phone call from an interior designer that I had met through networking. He liked my energy, and we got along like a house on fire. He told me he was just finishing up a penthouse that was going to be the best thing Naples has ever seen, and I should go see it. I was aware of his work but had not seen it live and in living color. I asked him if I could see it that day.

He said, "Yeah, my trucks are there now delivering the furniture."

I drove straight over to the property, and lo and behold, it was another WC property on the beach overlooking the Gulf. I go into the lobby, and the doorman was really professional. I gave him the name of the person I was given, and he directed me to the private elevator and told me to take it straight up to the twenty-second floor. The elevator doors opened into this beautiful custom-designed foyer, and all I could see was nothing but organized chaos going on. About fifty men and women were all running around with furniture, pillows, rugs, and plants, placing them in their prospective areas. I peeked in first and looked to my right. My eyes became fixated on this thick ceiling-to-floor glass-encased office with a wall of beautifully organized designer books and a large quartz tabletop desk with a big white supple leather chair behind it. I closed my eyes and said "*Oh my god*" underneath my breath because this was something to behold.

I was blown away by what I was seeing. Then I crept off the elevator as if I did not want anybody to know I was in the penthouse. When I turned to my left, I could not believe my eyes. The view was spectacular.

It was like you were walking in the middle of the Gulf of Mexico, and on a clear day, you could see from Marco Island to Naples and Naples to Fort Myers. As I walked around this massive, incredibly beautiful penthouse, the floors were intense. I had never seen anything like them before. Large, oversize slabs of three-by-six white porcelain tile with light-gray striations moving through them, indicative of a soft watercolor painting.

The tile ran through the entire interior and exterior of the penthouse.

Everything was of the highest quality: 11,698 square feet of nothing but fabulousness, and that was all under air. As I walked through every room, I had to take a deep breath. Large pieces of art with pops of color were on every wall. The furniture was pure luxury and modern with clean lines. The great room encompassed three seating areas with the focal point being in the middle of the room and in front of the incredible view. Positioned there was a massive glass dining table that sat fourteen people. The second area was for conversation, and the third was for the entertainment with a baby grand piano. Large sculptures adorned the throughways of the property along with life-size statues of silver abstract designs.

The kitchen was crazy amazing. The cabinets were beautiful exotic veneer wood with brushed nickel hardware. The appliances were Gaggenau. There were white quartz countertops throughout, thick glass table bases, and modern lighting.

It had four guest bedrooms that were set up like luxury hotel rooms, large and inviting. The bedding was luxury at its best. The master suite was the dazzler, though a masterpiece in itself. A tub fit for a goddess sitting in front of the Gulf of Mexico in all her glory!

This was what dreams were made of. I finally ran into the person I was supposed to ask for, and she could see it in my eyes.

All I could say was, "This is so badass," and we both started laughing.

After speaking about everything that was going on and what was about to happen at the property, I left to let her get on with her work.

As soon as I hit the outside of the building, I called the interior designer and said, "I don't care what you have to do, but I need to get this listing. Please get me in front of the client, and I will nail it and sell it."

He said, "Jane, I will do my best to get you an interview."

I could hardly contain myself, but I felt confident he would get me in front of them, and I would have to do the rest.

The next day, I was feeling really revved up and anxious. Something said to give a call to the $10-million penthouse customer and be a little more aggressive. Then I remembered my conversation with the interior designer. He shared with me that he had a program where if the customer's property was empty and the customer owned it outright with no mortgage, he would furnish it for one year, and once it sold, the customer would pay for the furnishings with no interest. Of course, the property would have to be sold furnished. I had it in my sixty-second pitch. I picked up the phone and dialed his number.

"Hello, hi, Mr. X——, this is Jane Bond calling you again."

"Hi, Jane," he said. *Did I detect a softness in his voice this time?* I said, "How are you?"

"Oh, I've been better.

"What can I do for you, Jane?"

"I'm calling you again because I have something that could get your property sold."

He started out with, "Jane, you agents——"

"Please, hear me out, Mr. X——. What if I told you I could have your place completely furnished without you putting a dime up front out of your pocket for a year?"

"Really? Jane, we are talking about a big place."

"I know, Mr. X——, but what if I could get it done? What do you think? Can I meet with you for thirty minutes? That's all I need of your time."

It was crickets for thirty seconds, and then he said, "What the hell. Come see me tomorrow at 2:00 p.m."

"Thank you, Mr. X——. I will see you then."

When I hung up the phone, I just screamed at the top of my lungs, *Yasss, Bond!* The timing could not have been better. We were just finishing up the seven-million-dollar listing and about to light it up on the MLS. I knew I had to nail this interview, so all night, I went over the letter that I had sent him like nobody's business and internalized every word. I was on cloud nine the next day and anxious as hell.

I drove over to Marco Island an hour early and parked in the lot waiting for the time to pass, repeating everything I was going to say out loud over and over. The phone rang, and it was Mr. X——. First thing I thought was, *Oh no, he's going to cancel.* It was just the opposite. He asked if I could come thirty minutes later. What a sigh of relief.

I said, "Of course, no problem, sir."

So there I sat in my car waiting, repeating what I was going to say and visualizing seeing my name on all three listings in the MLS. *HA!*

Fifteen minutes before the meeting, I started to drive down to the building, go through security, and into the lobby to wait for Mr. X——. All of a sudden, I saw an older woman walking over to me who actually looked a little like Phyllis Diller, somewhat eccentric. She introduced herself as Mrs. X——and told me that Mr. X—— was on his way in. As she and I sat and chatted for a few minutes, up came Mr. X——on this little scooter with one leg up.

What a lovely, sweet-looking older gentleman with a great smile.

Totally different than what I imagined. I won't get into what imagined. Just an Italian good ole boy. I could tell right away that he liked my energy and the way I carried myself. The first thing he did was compliment me on the way I dressed. We take the elevator up to the property and get off the elevator, right in the foyer of the penthouse.

They opened the large double doors, and wow! This place was almost identical to the sexy penthouse in Naples, but bigger: 16,894 square feet—3,000 feet more, and on the twenty-sixth floor, which seemed like we were way up in the sky. It was almost scary. Can you believe that?

Immediately, I started to think about things that we could do to make it more modern looking to get it sold if they were open to it. For starters, paint the entire property a light gray, and it would change the whole feel of the property and break up the traditional yellow-and-brown paint that was everywhere. But Mrs. X——was very proud of what she had done, especially the hideous huge brown oval marble inlay in the floor in the foyer, which set the tone as soon as you walked in. Also, there were yellow walls and deep-cream marble floors.

I did not want to offend her in any way. Mr. X——all of sudden blurted out that the reason he needed his scooter was because the place was simply too big for him to walk around. He proceeded to tell me he bought it because it was a deal at the time, and he thought his whole family would live there together at some point.

I said, "Funny, I hear this story a lot in my line of business, Mr. X——."

We all laughed, and he said, "Jane, the truth is, I don't want to pass away and leave Mrs. X——to deal with and sell this place on her own."

This penthouse was enormous and overwhelming—fit for a celebrity with an entourage, but in Marco, that would be a hard sell. We made our way back down to the lobby. Mr. X——immediately started asking me about real estate, how I got started, and where came from. I told him my story about my mom and dad being entrepreneurs and raising me and my siblings and how I started out selling distressed properties in the crash and worked my way up to being in his presence. I also shared with him that I was a former interior designer for pro athletes.

I asked him why he had an agent that was not even on his coast representing his property from a company with no reach. He said that he fed him this story about being international. I shared with him that my company was a true international company and we had one of the biggest networks internationally in the real estate industry. I told him that we also had the clientele already built in because of our auction houses all over the world and that his property could definitely be featured in them. Then I went in for the kill, sharing with him my marketing plan of action and the program the interior designer was offering.

I told him about the other penthouse in Naples and that I might be able to get him in to see it before he made his decision.

I could see he was impressed and excited.

He actually said, "You have me excited about selling this place again." The next words out his mouth was, "Let's do it. Leave the listing agreement with me, and I will sign it by tomorrow and call you to pick it up. I just need my attorney to look over a couple of things."

I didn't want to seem desperate, but I did ask if there was anything I could clarify for them. He turned to me and said no, with a slight grin. "I will get it back to you tomorrow afternoon," he said.

I gave Mrs. X——and Mr. X——a big hug and told them that they would not be disappointed. And just like that, I had two penthouses worth $18 million in the same building. I was floating on air driving back to my office. I called Frank and told him that I had gotten the listing.

He was like, "Really?"

I said, "Yes, babe."

I arrived back at the office, and as soon as I stepped foot into the office, Nick asked me, "How did it go?"

I closed my office door behind me, put my bags down, took a deep breath, and just started smiling, standing in front of the white board.

He said, "OMG, you got it!"

I said, "Yesssss, we got it!"

We started hugging each other and laughing out loud. After we calmed down, I wrote in the new listing for $10,000,000 on the whiteboard. I continued to just stand there and think about what it took to get here. Thinking this feeling was well worth it.

Next, I called my mother and told her the whole story, and she said, "Jane, you deserve it. You have worked really hard. I am so proud of you, Jannie, and blessed to have a child like you. If it was not for you making sure I had what I needed in this house, I don't know what I would have done. You always have been a go-getter, Jannie."

"Thank you, Mommy, but it ain't over yet. I'm praying I get this other listing or at least the opportunity to get in front of the seller. It's a long shot, Mom, but if I get the chance, I'm going to give it my best."

Chapter 10

# PLAYING IN THE SANDBOX

I had Nick start making phone calls, scheduling photography, video drone shots, 3-D walk through, floor plans, and looking at media partners we could utilize. Writing out copy for our properties was one of Nick's fortes. He had a way with words.

I turned to Nick and said, "Well, Nicky, all we have to do is nail down this last listing."

He said, "Yes, Ms. Bond. I'm praying you get the call so I can just see it."

All week, we were running around getting ready to release the new listing.

We had been at the penthouse most of the day for some last-minute pickup drone shots. When we got back to the office, I got the call I had been waiting for. At first, I sat there with my mouth wide open holding the phone. Nick looked at me and put his hand over his mouth.

It was a young lady on the other end of the phone with an Eastern European accent asking if I was Jane Bond. I said yes. She said that she worked for Mrs. Z——and she was calling to set up an interview with me. I wrote down the information and hung up the phone.

We looked at each other, and I started saying, "OMG, OMG, it is happening Nick."

We started talking about what it all meant and what it would be like to get this amazing listing along with having the two others. I told him I was taking him on the appointment with me and to be prepared. He was so excited. The appointment was set up for Tuesday of the following week, so we had plenty of time to prepare and do research.

That weekend, I looked up everything I could on Mrs. Z and her company. It was all pretty intimidating while reading it. I thought I was definitely in unchartered waters. I also looked at comps, and there were none, especially in the building. Nothing had sold in the building over $5 million in years. To make it even worse, I had never sold a multimillion-dollar property, even though I had just listed one. What I did have going for me was that I had a great track record for the past year with several-million-dollar property sales, twenty-six million dollars in listings going into the new season, a modern marketing plan of action, and a great personality. So I convinced myself I had a really good shot at nailing the interview. The day of the interview, we pulled the package together, and off we went to the property.

When we arrived, the doorman remembered me, and he was just as friendly as he wanted to be. I thought this a good sign.

Then a pretty young lady walked up to us. She spoke with an Eastern European accent, so I assumed she was the owner. She escorted us to the elevator but not the main elevator. She said she preferred that we take the domestics and workman elevator up. This elevator dropped us off in the outer hallways of the penthouse, a part of the penthouse I had not seen before. She explained that domestics would use this elevator and entry because it allowed them to enter the condo without going through the main part of the home with groceries and packages.

As we strolled around this sexy sky-high masterpiece of luxury, I was getting more and more excited.

I just blurted out and said, "I would do anything to have this listing. It is just so damn gorgeous. What do I have to do to get this listing?"

She and Nick looked at me and started laughing.

The young lady asked, "Do you think you can sell this condo?"

I said, "It will sell itself. It is that beautiful. Naples has never seen anything like this here before. This place is everything. I just could not contain my enthusiasm."

She smiled at me and said, "I like you and your assistant. You guys are a breath of fresh air. Youthful and funny." She shared with us that I was up against a couple of other agents, and then she asked me if I would put up window treatments on the window.

I said, "What for? Nobody can see you up here."

She started laughing, saying that another agent she interviewed suggested that.

I said, "Don't do anything else. The place is done. Please, I have to have this listing."

She said, "I will call you in a couple of days once Mrs. Z——— makes her decision."

I said, "Oh, you're not Mrs. Z———?"

"Oh, no, I am her liaison."

"Liaison, oh, okay, great," I said.

I thought, *Here it is. I'm just a little black girl from the hood, and now I'm standing in a multimillion-dollar penthouse, all decked out to the hill, talking to the liaison. Check that out. Wait till I share this with my mom.* LOL. All the way back to the office, we talked about the meeting and what we thought might change my entire career and put it on a whole other trajectory. The truth about the two other penthouses was that they were going to be a hard sell, but the real deal is, if you don't have them, then how in the hell can you sell them? My philosophy is, a try always beats a failure. And as long as I have them, can try to sell them and attract more business just by having them on my board. We carry on with the rest of the week with showings and prospecting, and of course, the only thing I keep thinking about is, *When are we going to get the call?*

The weekend passed, and we were back at work Monday morning. The call came in, and it was the young lady.

She said, "Jane."

I said, "Yes."

She said, "This is the liaison for Mrs. Z———."

I could hardly breathe.

Her next words were, "Mrs. Z——has chosen you to sell the penthouse. Please send us the listing agreement."

I said, "Yes, so what is the price they decided on?"

She said, "$16,995,000."

*Holy cow!* I hung up, and Nick and I just started screaming and jumping around. I just sealed my brand and position as a top agent with $42 million in listings.

I rushed downstairs into my broker's office to share with him the amazing news. I sat down in his office, and he said, "Yes," with a big smile as he normally did with me.

"I have some incredible news, Chris. I just landed a $16,995,000 listing!"

He said, "You are kidding."

"No, I'm not."

I told him the story, and he said, "I knew you could do this. When can I see?"

"Chris, this is the most beautiful listing we ever had in this office. Wait until you see this place, Chris."

He asked me if I believed in the price. I told him I thought it should be $15,995,000. Two minutes later, my phone rang, and it was the liaison. She told me that Mrs. Z——'s husband just came back in town and he decided to raise the price because it was too low. He wanted it raised to $17,995,000.

I almost fell off the chair. Now, how was I going to pull this off?

It was now $2,000,000 over the suggested retail. I looked at Chris, and he told me that I needed to try to talk them out of raising the price that high.

I said, "Don't think I can, but come and see the place, and then you tell me."

I immediately called the seller's liaison back and tried to share with her my thoughts on the price. I told her that we should really reconsider putting this property on the market at a lower price point. She told me that Mrs. Z——and her husband believed in the price they offered and that was what they wanted.

We as agents definitely are the informed experts when it comes to pricing property because we are out here in the field on a daily basis, not only with our ears to the ground, but also pricing property every day with what the market will bear. On the other hand, I knew that this property was going to solidify my career as a top agent who lists million-dollar properties. So I never mentioned lowering the price again to my customers or the liaison. As soon as the property went up on the company board with the other two, the $7 million and $10 million, the frenzy began. Once I presented my marketing plan of action to the sellers, that was when I realized it was a different type of ball game, one I had no idea about. They were vetting every photographer, magazine, and the type of launch party I was proposing. This was very different than what was used to. The Marco Island sellers were not this intense. It was like they were calling all the shots. What I did learn was that I needed to clearly upgrade my standards in the future because this was a different level and I had to level up!

I don't know any other agent in Naples that has done it better since.

Hello, Top Agent Jane Bond! Now it was time to get to work. We were in full motion with the two Marco properties. Mr. X——, the $10-million client, declined the offer of the interior designer. Staging or even painting the property was out of the question. So what we came up with was having oversize renderings created and a seventy-five-inch flat screen in the condo with virtual renderings looping as prospective buyers viewed the property. We found that buyers spent more time in the space with this. The smaller penthouse was getting quite a bit of traffic because it was partially furnished and we did the same with the virtual staging.

We also were able to put the virtual staging photos on the MLS, which was a plus as long as we disclosed that the photos were virtual renderings. This garnered more interest as opposed to having empty room photos. I got on the horn and called everybody—all my media partners: *Mansion Global,* the *New York Times, Gulfshore Life Magazine, Home and Design Magazine, Fine Magazine,* etc. I lined them up to come and view the new property along with my broker. One, to see who was excited about the property, and two, to see who wanted to give us a big enough ad for free. I called the press so we could get on TV or the early news because I knew they were always looking for content, and my timing could not have been better.

The largest lottery jackpot ever was on the line, so the alignment of that and a $18,000,000 luxury penthouse was on point. The storyline was, *What could you buy with a $100 million dollars?*

Next, I had Nick put together an international personal e-mail blast to send out to all of Sotheby's top agents around the world.

From the top agents I had met in my travels to Europe, I simply picked up the phone to call them and share with them personally, creating buzz throughout the company, not only with my name but my listings. The momentum was incredible. I was moving through things like a freight train.

We received a phone call from the interior designer about scheduling photography. He wanted to know if I could have someone meet his photographer at the penthouse to shoot. I told him that I would meet him there personally. He proceeded to ask me if I wanted to use his photographs once they were done and that I should because his photographer shot for *AD, Architecture Digest*.

I said, "Are you joking?"

He said, "No, why not, Jane? You would want the highest-quality photographs for this place," and he was right.

And I already had pushed back from the sellers on the photographers I referred to them. This was godsent. Needless to say, the photographs came out beyond beautiful.

Everyone was talking about the eighteen-million-dollar penthouse.

*Gulfshore Life Magazine* had been good to me in the past, writing stories about me starring in the pilot of *Naples Housewives* and on my success as an agent climbing to the top. So I thought it was only fitting to give them the story. *Gulfshore* did right by me. I received an eight-page spread in the magazine. I also had a story in *Mansion Global, Naples Daily News*, and *Florida Weekly*. Not a bad start. The sellers were happy, and so was Sotheby's.

Now came the big reveal to the public about the launch party. Everybody wanted to come to the party, and the sellers wanted the list to see if I was connected enough to invite people that could possibly afford this property. So again, Nick and I put on our thinking caps and started on the phones.

The first thing I said to Nick was, "I need a damn sponsor. This is going to cost me a fortune."

When you're a listing agent, you definitely need a marketing budget to pull shit like this off.

A property of this magnitude had to be introduced to the public with a bang, and the only way to do that for this type of property is to launch it for takeoff!

This launch party was going to cost a pretty penny, because I had to invite wealthy people, and they were used to the best of all things. So why not get my bank involved, which was a wealth management bank, who not only could sponsor me but had a built-in clientele with plenty of money? #Boom. I thought, *Yes, of course they do, but I want them to pay for everything.* I'd been to the bank's Christmas parties and seen and met some of their customers. This was definitely the right brand alignment. I decided to call them and set up a meeting. I got big Mike Giusto, the manager on the phone, knowing that this was some next-level shit. I told him all about the penthouse and how I thought this would be a great event for us to join forces on. I knew he did not have the last word, so I had to sell it to him to take back to the decision maker. As I was speaking to him, I could tell he was getting very psyched and called the meeting right away. We got in for a meeting, and we were escorted into a conference room in a part of the bank I had never been in. Awaiting us in the conference room is a whole setup.

Shrimp, salads, sandwiches, fruits, coffee, tea, and even wine.

*Whoa*, I thought, *this is how you get treated at this level? I like it.*

There are a couple of people at the meeting besides Michael that I was familiar with. We were asked if we wanted anything to eat or drink. I was almost embarrassed to say yes because I was about to ask them to pay for everything. We started the meeting by pitching them the whole scenario for the event. Having at least two hundred people, including press, *Gulfshore Life*, the interior designer, director of Sotheby's for Southwest Region, fifty of the top agents in Naples, and the rest of wealthy clientele that could possibly afford the property.

I shared with them that the reason I thought they were a good fit was that they were a wealth management bank and had been my bank for several years, so it only made sense to align myself with them and Sotheby's for this event. They asked what was needed from them.

I said, "Frankly, pay for everything."

"And what does that entail?"

Michael asked. "Catering, entertainment, valet service, and swag. If you would like to invite some of your own clientele, that would be a good look for the bank," I said.

I also told them that we would give them signage on all marketing and put their swag in our gift bags. We were already being provided beautiful luxury swag bags from the designer.

We made our way over to the penthouse after the meeting and all of the bank's reps were blown away. They could not catch their breath and immediately said they would do it. We were all set. What a triumphant day for me. Yeah! We started putting our guest list together for the who's who in Naples and sending them out. Pulling it all together was not as difficult as we thought it was going to be. Just a little nerve-wracking waiting for the RSVP count and reporting back to the sellers what guests were confirmed.

The launch party was a hit. Everyone showed up on the list.

The most interesting part of the night was when I was saying hello to the guests, a lady walked up to me with an accent and said, "They tell me you are someone I should meet."

I said, "Really? Well, hello, I am Jane Bond, the listing agent for the property."

She said, "It is nice to meet you," with a very heavy Eastern European accent. "My name is Mrs. Z——."

I looked at her again, blinked, grabbed her, and gave her a hug. I said, "I want to say thank you so much for believing in me to represent your amazing property. Are you pleased with the turnout?"

She looked around and said, "Yes, everything looks lovely, Jane."

The cameras were flickering, interviews were being done in different corners of the property, wine was flowing, candles glowing, and the pianist was playing great music all through the evening. The guests loved the property and talked among themselves, discussing who they could tell about the property that might be interested. As the night started winding down, we stood at the door to say good night to people and make sure they took their gift bags. Filled with plenty of good swag, champagne, chocolates, beautiful magazines, and a copy of the property's portfolio and info.

The last guest left at 1:00 a.m. Can you say success? It was definitely one for the books. A couple of days later, I got a call from the manager of the building asking me to please stop by his office because he wanted to talk to me about something. I stopped by his office during lunch to see what he wanted to ask me. He asked if I would do a private building showing for the neighbors. I told him I would have to ask Mrs. Z——for permission but I was sure it would be okay. I actually thought it was a good idea because this way, I could meet the rest of the neighbors that lived in the building. There was not one condo in the building under $4 million, so this was right up my alley, and I had quite a few gift bags left that I gave to guests as parting gifts. People love gift bags. Meeting the neighbors was really informative. They stressed to me how important the sale of the penthouse was because it would raise the value of the building and awareness of the area. I spoke with one neighbor who was the head of the board, and he said that people did not even know where the area was located, even though it was located on the beach and behind one of the most expensive open-air malls in the city. I found that hard to believe.

Selling is selling, all day long, no matter what!

Marketing is so essential to your business and for selling a product in today's world of instant gratification and social media. Usually, the rule of thumb as a marketing budget was 10 percent. In this case, thank God a lot of media outlets provided free marketing for this place. You do the math.

Your message has to be targeted and attention grabbing because you only have sixty seconds in some cases. Your audience is just like the movie *Gone in 60 seconds*. I put on my thinking cap and said, *What could I do differently to sell this property properly and garner interest to the area?*

Chapter 11

................................................

# SELLING A ROCK STAR

When I lived in NYC, I was an entertainment manager and always had to come up with ideas to promote my clients. So now, I looked at this property as a rock star. *How do you sell a rock star, Jane?* I decided to do an introduction video and personally drive the area and walk through the property and commentate. Since this was a luxury property in a high-end area, it was a no-brainer. Picture this, me driving in a black on black trimmed-in-white-interior Rolls-Royce Ghost narrating the lifestyle of the area, driving through the open-air mall where Louis Vuitton, Gucci, Saks, Tiffany, and Salvatore Ferragamo live.

Also, I drove near Artis-Naples, where Broadway plays and ballets are held, in addition to music performances by A-list artists like Harry Connick Jr. and Tony Bennet. I continue to narrate, driving through the secret garden up to the clearing of the building as the footage cut to me in the penthouse, walking through the property highlighting and pointing out everything that the interior designer did to bring this masterpiece to fruition. I tell you, no one had done anything like this before in my market—produced a video of a listing and narrated it. The agents, interior designers, and sellers all bought it, hook line and sinker.

It became a great promotional tool for all involved.

Not only did I blow it out of the water, I upped my brand tenfold.

You can watch the videos here:

https://www.youtube.com/watch?v=JSQd
zIlx8Ko
https://www.239listing.com/property-florida/
sky-high-luxury-naples-penthouse

Now, I just have to sell this baby! Everything was in place. Our first showing was from an agent with a fake buyer. You can always tell. I had heard that I had won the listing over this agent and several other top agents. The funny thing was that none of these same agents ever showed the property once; the whole time it was on the market. I don't know if that is trying to lock you out of attaining top-dog status or pure jealousy, especially when you don't look like them in any shape, form, or fashion. They did not even support me by show-ing up. I found that a little hurtful, and I knew they clearly had the clientele that could afford it.

The one thing that I've learned in this business is that you can-not trust anyone. Not broker, colleague, family member, friend, or the little old couple. They will throw your ass underneath the bus with the quickness and ask that you put skin in the game after the fact. I say keep your eyes open, ear to the ground, and mouth shut at all times. Money changes people. Six months passed by, and no offers came in. However, my customer still believed in me and renewed the listing agreement for another six months. The feedback was that the property was not worth the money it was being offered at $17.995 million. It was not only the sale of the property the buyer had to endure; it was also the $200,000 in yearly fees to keep the property, and that included your real estate taxes.

I knew in my heart that the value was in my initial suggested price to seller, with room to negotiate $16.5 million.

I started to think about how I was able to get the seven-mil-lion-dollar referral by networking on the other coast and interview-ing with other brokerages. I thought, *Maybe I should revisit some of those conversations, in particular, that startup Compass.* This company was very technology based, which could give me a bigger reach with their systems and tools. Not only that, their fresh, new, and contemporary brand aligned with the way the housing market was trending. I also interviewed with the NYC hip and slick Douglas Elliman. However, I'm not going to say that I was not drawn to DE because of its glossy look and cool agents. I definitely was. Being at Sotheby's, I felt trapped in a time zone with everything, and none of my listings were moving. I thought about it for a week and decided to contact the brokers again and see what they had to offer. I was already driving back and forth. Now it was about making a serious move to upgrade my business and stay committed.

Nick and I drove over to Miami the next week and met with Douglas Elliman and Compass. On the drive back from Miami, we both decided Compass was the company to go with to grow my brand. I felt like we would be in good hands. But I knew I could not just up and leave Sotheby's. They were definitely not going to allow me to take my listings without a fight. So I had to put my plan together to leave, which meant going to my customers first to tell them I was leaving, and then tell Sotheby's. I thought, if my customers didn't have an issue with me parting ways with Sotheby's, then that would be a good thing because that would mean they believed in me and my ability to get their property sold, irrespective of my brokerage.

Another ninety days passed by, and now we were in the dead of August. Ninety-nine-degree weather and humidity, hot as hell. Now, I was getting really anxious and bothered, so decided to make the move before the season started back up again and I had to extend my listings under Sotheby's.

In October, I left Sotheby's to sign with Compass. I was able to take my listings with me except for one, the ten-million-dollar listing. Ugh, you could have killed me right there and then. Ten million dollars, cut from your listing bank pipeline can be painful to your future earnings. For the four months Sotheby's had the listing after I left, they did not sell it, and my customer signed a new listing agreement with Compass. Can you say market share? Compass got a $10,000,000 listing, and I got an opportunity to sell it again.

It took me about thirty days to get acclimated and settled in, but I loved it! The new brand fit like a glove. The marketing and advertising had a modern, fresh, and clean look about it. My customers seemed to love the new feel and look of the company. We had no complaints.

I decided to try to broach the subject with the liaison about a possible price adjustment, and that turned out to be a flat out NO from the seller. A customer came out of the woodwork that seemed somewhat promising, and at the same time, I had someone inquiring about the seven-million-dollar listing on Marco that turned out to be a lead that went nowhere. The prospective buyer wanted to do a trade but was unrealistic on the value of his home and really did not have the cash to close the deal. That was very disappointing. The lead for Mrs. Z's property turned out to be a single hedge-fund guy that was just a lot of talk trying steal the property.

We had a couple of weird inquiries. One guy called and said he was interested in the ten-million-dollar penthouse and turned out to be a weirdo.

He had been calling me for a while asking me all kinds of questions about the property, giving us the story that his family was into old vintage movies and that was how they made their fortune. He had been looking at this property for quite some time, and it was perfect for his extended family.

Also, he loved the fact that it was close to the private airport for the family jet and that we needed to research a place where they could keep the family's 110-feet yacht. What made me suspicious was, he did not have an agent, and when I asked for proof of funds, he said that he wasn't accustomed to sending out his information before seeing the property. I said that was all well and fine, but when he knew his schedule to come to Naples, either send it before he arrived or bring it with him since I was the listing agent. We started googling this guy and could not find anything on him.

The scary thing was that we found a convicted sex offender with a criminal record in Lakeland, Florida, with the same name. How scary is that?

The next week, this guy called again and said that he would be in Naples this week and wanted to see the place. Again, I asked him for proof of funds, and this time he said he would send it. Well, we never received it, and he never showed up. As a female agent, we have to be very careful out here today. I can't even imagine what this guy had in mind. Thank God all my properties are in gated communities. When anyone arrives, a guard at the gate gets your license plate number and the doorman takes a copy of your driver's license.

These buildings usually have heavy security and cameras everywhere.

The season was upon us again, and the people were rolling in from the North, Midwest, and Europe. You would see the car caravans unloading Rolls-Royce, Maseratis, and Mercedes at the end of different wealthy communities. Restaurants were filling up, and the beaches were full. It was the season again, and I was nervous as hell because my listing was about to expire and I had no offers as of yet. What was even worse, Nick decided he wanted to leave Naples, which meant leaving me. I did not want to lose him because I trusted him more than anyone I had worked with in the past. However, I understood he moved here from DC right out college. We would often have the conversation about him living in a predominantly older, retired city.

He missed his friends terribly, and he wanted to travel. I couldn't blame him.

He was too young to stay in Naples at this time in his life. The day he left, we cried together in the office as he packed up his things, and off he went. We are still very close and talk often.

Chapter 12

# WHO'S THE REAL BALLER?

The Christmas season rolled back around, and to my surprise, I was given another six-month extension by Mrs. Z——and I was elated. I was not interested in another agent getting the opportunity to benefit from all my hard work, which could have easily happened. Think about it. I had done all the heavy lifting already. Press, videos, magazines, photography, and the parties. I definitely would've been sick. But this just fueled me to do more and try to attract my buyer. I began to roll out the marketing a little heavier. Not doing anything new, but just reinforcing what I had already done over the course of the year. I had to get this property sold. All I could think of was, *It's one thing, Jane, to get the listing. It is quite another to sell it.* I started losing a little faith that this would happen. Every time I thought I was close to a good lead, it would not pan out. I decided to go see my mother for a few days with the hope that this would make me feel better.

While I was in Philly, I got a call from an agent that asked me how negotiable I thought Mrs. Z——was when it came to selling the penthouse. He said he had a customer that was interested in the property and was considering putting an offer in. I asked if the customer had seen the property. He said yes. Initially, he tried to cajole me into giving him a number. Then he started throwing crazy, unrealistic numbers out, asking me if I thought Mrs. Z would be interested in taking it. After going back and forth a few times, I ended up telling him if I were him, I would just put an offer in and we would go from there. I have to admit, I got a little excited thinking about bringing Mrs. Z——an offer. He told me he would get back to me if they wanted to put an offer in.

I didn't discuss this with anyone because I had been down this road a few times already and never received an offer. Two days later, I got another call from the agent, and the buyers wanted to see the property, and of course, I was out of town. This is always the way. I explained to him that I was out of town but would have someone show the property to his buyers. *Fuck!* No one could show that property but myself or Nick. There were so many bells and whistles; one of us had to be there, and that was not happening. Nick did not work for me anymore, nor did he live in Naples, and I was out of town. I called my husband right away and explained everything to him and asked if he thought he could handle it, and he said yes. I told him that I could be on the phone with him as he walked the buyers through the penthouse.

The next day, the agent showed up with his buyers, and everything went well. I did have the opportunity to speak with the agent and his customers while they were there. I explained to the agent over the phone that I would be back next week and could show them everything the penthouse really had to offer. He was very pleasant at that time and said they were good for now. That evening, the agent called me and said that they were going to put an offer in.

I could have fainted. This was music to my ears. I was on pins and needles for the next two days waiting for the offer to come. I flew back to Naples, and when I stepped off the plane, I heard a text come through, and it was from the agent telling me he e-mailed me the offer. I stopped dead in my tracks, put my bags down, and went straight to my e-mails. I looked at the offer, and you know how you get that feeling in the pit of your stomach that something is about to happen and it ain't good. That was me all day long. Rolling my eyes would be an understatement. I kept telling myself, *Jane, this is just a start*, but we were so far apart, and no matter what, I knew I had to present this offer to Mrs. Z——by law.

I called the liaison and shared with her that we had an offer but it ain't good. She asked that I send it over anyway. The response was no response. The buyers walked away. In our business, when a seller does not give you a response, it usually means that they were insulted by the offer.

To say this was a disappointment is to put it mildly. I thought that we would have at least danced a couple of times. I thought, *Okay, Jane, season is in full swing, and that is the first offer of the new season. At least we had an offer come in. That in itself is promising, so snap out of it, girl.*

Two weeks later, I got a call from a familiar-looking number, and it was the agent with the lowball offer. I answered the phone like we were old friends, and he responded in the same manner. We started to discuss what went down with the last offer and how his buyers were not interested in paying anything more than that. I shared with him that I was shocked that his customer would even present and offer such as that for my listing. Now I knew this was going to be a cat-and-mouse game. He proceeded to ask me again what I thought Mrs. Z——would take at this point. I wasn't even sure because she gave no indication from the offer. Nor would the liaison give me any indication. I really didn't think she had a clue either. Again, he told me he would get back to me.

A few hours later, I get an e-mail from the agent, and I couldn't wait to open it. I just knew it would be much closer. I was like, *OMG, this shit is not going to fly either.* Now I was beginning to think these buyers were not serious. I called the agent and asked him what was going on, and he told me that my customers were crazy to think they were going to get anywhere near their number.

I told him, "Well, it definitely will not be your customer that will be purchasing this property then."

I left off sharing with him that I would present the offer but that they shouldn't expect too much. This offer just annoyed my seller, and she countered with a five-hundred-dollar reduction, which was a slap in the face. My seller was so pissed that she said she didn't want to entertain another offer from the buyers.

Now we were talking about millions of dollars, and they were definitely not playing monopoly. I had to take a step back because this was a big money game. When I went back to the agent and shared with him the counter, he became furious, and I started seeing another side of him somewhat. He said his customer was not going to come up. I urged him that if they wanted this property, they were going to have get serious and bring us a realistic offer.

A week passed by, and I didn't hear from the agent. Another week went by and nothing. Then I got a call from the agent. Now I was getting really excited. He told me that the customer wanted to come and view the condo again before putting in another offer. I welcomed this because now I could meet the buyers in person and also show them everything this incredible property had to offer. We set up the showing for the next day at 1:00 p.m. It could not come fast enough for me. All night, I was fantasizing about how this could change not only my career, but my life.

This type of payday is life-changing for any agent, at any stage of his or her career. I try not to go there because you are only setting yourself up for a huge letdown. But what the hell? Just the thought of it was a roller-coaster ride.

The agent arrived early, and we go up to the condo and walked around. I showed him a few things, and he got a call to go down to collect his buyers. I greeted them at the elevator inside the penthouse. I had the music playing throughout the property and began my tour. I told them all about how the designer gutted the property and put his star power stamp on it by adorning it with three-by-five slabs of Italian porcelain tile throughout the interior and exterior of the entire property and chose the finest furnishings from Italy. I also showed them the Crestron system that controlled the entertainment system and lighting, which was LED. The kitchen was outfitted with all Gaggenau appliances, the cabinetry with exotic veneer wood and quartz countertops.

I saw that they were in awe. I showed them how the iPad controlled everything in the property.

The buyer turned to me and said, "I feel like I know you. I have watched your video of the property with you in it at least a hundred times."

I continued to show them all the amenities the building had to offer, including the cabana. Yes, the property had its own cabana, a one-bedroom apartment on the first floor of the building where the new owners could hang out while at the beach or the pool. After showing them the garage, we said our goodbyes and parted ways.

I felt great after that showing, and I knew I nailed it. The next day, the agent called me and said that they were pleased with the showing and were going to submit another offer. I hung up and started calling Frank, my best friend John, and my mom. Frank told me not to count the money until it was in the bank. I know that is the rule of thumb.

My best friend John was like, "Holy shit, girlfriend. Bond, this is huge, right?"

I said, "This is going to change my whole business and life in one breath."

John has been my best friend for thirty years, so he was rooting for me and has watched me work to get to this point forever. I had to share it with him.

My mom just very sweetly said, "I am going to pray for you, baby."

Shit, I needed everyone to pray for me. LOL. I was getting physically sick waiting for this offer to come in. Four days had passed by, and I had not heard from the agent. I waited another day and called him. He explained to me that the buyer had gone out of town and he was going to submit the offer today. *Ugh, thank you, God!*

The offer finally came in, and it was better, but I was thinking not good enough.

And boy was I right. This offer really pissed my seller off—to the point that she drafted a not-so-nice e-mail and asked that I send it to the buyer's agent and insisted that he deliver it to his customer. *This is not good,* I was thinking. *There goes everything down the goddamn drain, including my status change, commission, and the listing.* I was about to lose my freaking mind.

This is a horrible position to be in. I had to grab ahold of myself because I was becoming a nervous wreck. This shit was depressing, and I was freaking out somewhat because of what was at stake. When I read the e-mail, I knew this was going to be explosive and send the buyers walking. This was definitely a power struggle mixed with ego and a lot of crazy money. Well, I sent over the e-mail, and of course, that pissed the buyers right off, and they walked. I went into a mild depression. I could not sleep from thinking about what happened and did not have another prospect in sight. My other two properties were not getting any traffic at all.

Frank was going to Chicago for business and suggested I go with him. I thought that was a great idea. I love Chicago, and this would take my mind off things, and eventually, I would feel better. We have friends in Chicago that are in real estate, and they invited me out to lunch. While at lunch, they asked me about the deal, and I gave them blow by blow. They were really surprised we could not close the deal.

They said, "Sometimes, that is par for the course."

Five days had passed since the deal blew up, and I had pretty much written it off for good. At this point, I was miserable. None of my multimillion-dollar properties were under contract, and the expiration date was getting closer.

I went back to our beautiful hotel, the Peninsula, to relax and wait for my husband to finish his meeting. As soon as I lay down, the phone rang. I looked at the phone, and lo and behold, it was the buyer's agent.

I jumped up and went into the bathroom and started pacing the floor, nervous as all hell. I didn't answer the phone. I guess I wanted to think about my tone before I took his call. I had been in the dumps for days, over this deal falling the hell apart, but shit, I did not want him to know that. So I waited for him to call back.

Frank came back to the hotel room, and I told him what had just happened, and then the phone rang again. It was him, the agent.

"Hello, Jane," the agent said, speaking as if I did not know who was calling. He leaned right in on me, real hardcore about the price of the property and reiterating that we would never sell the property for what we wanted and my sellers needed to really reconsider his buyers' last offer. He also shared with me how offended they were by the e-mail. I thought about it for a minute. I don't think he even gave them that e-mail because if so, the buyers would have never come back, in my opinion. I told him that we were all working for the same goal here. However, this would have to be a win-win situation for both parties and if his buyers wanted this property, they would have to come up significantly.

He said he would try to talk to them but was not going to make any promises. I called Mrs. Z——directly this time and spoke to her in depth about the deal possibly coming back together, trying to gauge where she was and what her thoughts might be. She turned around and asked me what did I think was a fair number. I gave her my opinion of the time factor being on the market, the number of offers, and no price reduction.

Some buyers will not put an offer in when they see that there has not been any movement from the seller on the price.

We proceeded to wait for the next move. I began to feel sick, paralyzed, and numb from sitting on the cold granite in the bathroom the whole time we had been negotiating.

It must have not been more than forty-five minutes, and I received another offer. I called Mrs. Z——immediately. She requested that I send it to her right away. She came right back to me with another counter. I sent it over to the agent without calling him.

He called me within a heartbeat and said, "What is this, Jane?"

"Look, this is what my seller wants, and that's that. Do what you need to do to get your customer up. We are very close."

He came back to me within the hour with another counter. I sent it right over. I wasn't even speaking with the liaison now. I took complete control and started dealing directly with Mrs. Z——. It had been difficult not communicating with Mrs. Z——directly. Now, I had her full attention.

This time she called me and said, "I will give them an answer tomorrow, and, Jane, if they do not accept my counter, I will not deal with them anymore."

*Counter! Another counter, OMG! This is not going to fly. They are not expecting another counter.* I was freaking out. We were so close. This could not possibly blow up again. I told Frank we needed to go out tonight so I could drink because I was losing my mind. I knew I was not going to sleep anyway. I was completely stressed out and consumed with this deal. No amount of alcohol was going to stop me from thinking about this deal. The whole night at dinner, I talked about the negotiations with Frank. I knew he kind of knew what number Mrs. Z——was looking for, but she was being very methodical in her negotiating, especially when she informed me that she would get back to the buyers tomorrow. I did not see that coming. I thought I had two vodka martinis at dinner but felt nothing. My energy was off the Richter scale.

That morning, I woke up fairly early and checked my e-mails right away and nothing. I thought, *Fuck, how long is this going to play itself out today?* I would be on a plane in a few hours. I lay in the bed with my eyes wide open, replaying yesterday in my head blow by blow, thinking how intense it was.

I felt this heavy sinking feeling coming over me. I was really letting this deal consume me to the point that I was scared as hell and becoming very depressed.

I said, *No, Jane, get your ass up and start packing. Whatever is going to happen is going to happen.* Actually I was talking to myself out loud, "You can't miss anything you never had. So snap the hell out of it." I have always been a fighter and a very positive person, but this was different.

Our flight did not leave until 4:00 p.m., so we decided to pack up and leave our bags at the reception and go to lunch.

It was a gorgeous day in Chicago. While at lunch, I forced myself not to talk about the deal and tried to enjoy lunch with Frank. As we were walking back to the hotel, I got a call from Mrs. Z——. I told her I was on the street and would be back in the hotel, where it was quiet, in five minutes and would give her a callback.

We got back to the hotel, and I quickly returned Mrs. Z——'s call.

"Hi, Jane," she said in her very soft voice but strong accent. "I am sending this counter back over to you, and I want you to send it to the buyer's agent with a message."

I was thinking, *Aw, shit, this is not going to be good.* When I get really nervous, I start to itch, and right at that moment, I started to itch and have a hot flash at that same time.

She continued to say, "You tell the agent that if I do not hear back from them, only with acceptance of my counter by the end of day, I will be putting the property back on the market at its original price, and their dealings with me are completely over."

I didn't know how I managed to answer her because right at that moment, I was about to vomit. I said "Yes, Mrs. Z———. I will let them know immediately."

I hung up the phone and could not speak. I was too afraid to look at the counter. So I told Frank to look at the contract and tell me the number.

I was holding my breath when he blurted it out.

I said, "Repeat that, baby." He repeated the number. I thought, *That's not so bad.* If the buyers don't take this, then they never wanted the property. I called the agent with a renewed confidence. I felt the price Mrs. Z———came to was fair market value for this incredible property. I told him what Mrs. Z had asked me to relay to him.

He took in what I said without any resistance, which was surprising since he had been so strong with me yesterday and days before. Maybe he was just as outdone as I was with the negotiations. He just said he would get back to me before 5:00 p.m. I told him that I would be on a plane at 4:00 p.m. and would like to hear from him preferably before my departure and hung up.

Literally forty minutes later, my phone rang, and it was the agent. "Hello, Jane, are you sitting down?"

I replied, "Yes, I'm actually in a cab on my way to the airport."

The next words out his mouth was, "We have a deal."

I thought my heart stopped for a moment.

He said, "Are you there?"

I said, "I can't hear you. Can you repeat that?"

"I said we have a deal," he repeated.

Right at that moment, I started blinking to see if I was awake but still numb. *Snap out of it, Jane. This is great!*

"Listen, I will be on the plane for the next two and a half hours, but I will have Internet. Please get me the fully executed contract before 5:00 p.m., okay?"

"No problem. Will do," he said.

I hung up and looked at Frank and said, "They accepted Mrs. Z——'s counter. I can't freaking believe it. This is amazing!"

Now, I just wanted that signed contract in my hands. I called Mrs. Z——to give her the good news, but she did not seem bothered one iota.

She simply said to me, "Let's see if we get the contract back by five today, or it's off."

I thought, *Oh my. Okay, this is how the game is played at this level.* No excitement, no emotion. Just contracts and dollars.

I must have checked my e-mail every five minutes, praying that I get the contract before boarding the plane and getting seated.

Ten minutes into the flight, I got the e-mail with the signed contract. I can't tell you what a sigh of relief it was to see that e-mail come across my phone.

I put my head back on the seat and whispered, "Thank you, God!"

Frank looked at me and said, "Well done, baby. Well done."

When the flight attendant asked me what I wanted to drink, I said, "A glass of wine, and keep my glass full all the way to Florida please." I fell asleep after the first glass of wine.

The next morning, I went into the office and started pulling together all the paperwork. Listing agreement, sales contract, disclosures, and condo documents to send to the agent and lawyers. This was an all-cash deal, closing in ten days without an inspection. Can you ask for a better deal?

I informed the manager of the building to get the board together to approve the buyers. He was so excited for the building and said he was going to do everything in his power to get the buyers approved quickly. I knew all the neighbors would be happy, especially the board because they had stressed to me during the private showing that they needed this property to sell.

This meant that the neighbors could sell their condos for a premium now because of the penthouse comp. Some neighbors might have to do some upgrading, but I was sure they wouldn't mind.

The buyers wanted to go back to the penthouse and walk around one last time, to create a punch list and familiarize themselves with the workings of the appliances, electronics, and A/C. The walkthrough lasted for about three hours. The buyers pulled out every drawer, pulled every handle, clicked every remote, turned every knob, and opened and shut every door before they left. The next morning, we received their punch list and got the handyman to take care of it all. Now, we just waited to close.

It was March 2017, closing day. I woke up really early and got dressed, had coffee with Frank, and drove down to the penthouse. I took the private elevator up, walked into the penthouse, and parked myself in the living area, looking out at the Gulf of Mexico as far as I could see. This was the biggest day of my real estate career. I was scared to death and sitting there completely numb. Because I knew that this deal was very volatile and at any minute, it could all go right down the fucking drain, along with my career of becoming a top listing agent in my market.

The buyers had walked away four times during negotiations. All I could do was sit there thinking what would it be like if this deal fell apart and how would I put it back together again. Mrs. Z——— had already expressed to me that she was not willing to deal with the buyers' shit anymore, so this deal had to close. There would be no coming back to the table. No one knew I was at the penthouse, only Frank. I didn't even know why I was at the penthouse. I just felt the need to be there.

It was approaching three thirty in the afternoon and nothing yet. I thought, *What could be taking so damn long? This was a cash deal.* Finally, I picked up the phone and called my mother and told her where I was and what was going on. I asked her to pray for me because I wanted this deal that bad and needed it. She said okay and hung up. I decided to walk around the penthouse, and as I walked into the kitchen, I heard the sound of an e-mail coming through. I ran back to my phone, and there it was: "WE ARE CLOSED." I could not believe my eyes. I looked at my watch, and it was 4:45 p.m. I literally sat there for nine hours. I packed up my bags, put the keys on the counter, took one last long look at the view, turned all the lights out, and left.

On the drive home, I thought, *What is going to happen now? I'm sure there will be some press on this, but I will have to deal with it tomorrow. I am exhausted.*

I got home and told Frank that we had closed.

He said, "What are you going to do now?"

I said, "Go to bed."

This had been a very trying day. I thought I was kind of in shock and needed to lie down from all the anxiety. I slept like a baby for the first time in a month.

As soon as I got up, the phone started to ring with press calling and wanting to interview me. *Naples Daily News, Black Enterprise, Gulfshore Life Magazine, Curb Magazine*, the *Real Deal*, and *Mansion Global*. They all ran stories on the sale. It was amazing because I still was not excited about the sale. I went into the office like it was any other day. Only this time, my name was on the sale side of the board with CLOSED on it. The whole office knew, and that was when it really hit me. I did it! I had just sealed my career forever more by breaking the biggest record in Naples. I sold the largest, most expensive penthouse on the beach ever. And today, I still hold that record and sell million-dollar properties in Naples.

The moral of this book, agents, is that if I could do it, you can do it. All it takes is hard work, consistency, a lot of follow-up, a little bit of luck, and knowing your *big why*. And you too can become the next million-dollar listing agent in your market.

# ACKNOWLEDGMENTS

I would like to thank my mom, Geraldine Bond, for her love and patience. She always encouraged me to dream big and to live my life without any regrets. I love you forever, Mom! Greene would be very proud. You did a great job.

LUXURY LIFESTYLE LIVING
Seasons at Naples Cay • Naples, Florida

Premier | Sotheby's
INTERNATIONAL REALTY

**Seasons at Naples Cay**
81 Seagate Drive #2201
Naples, FL 34103

- 11,698 square feet under air
- 13,624 total square feet
- 360-degree views
- 31 x 72 Italian porcelain flooring
- LED recessed lighting and versatile LED Kreon
- Custom millwork in exotic real wood veneers
- Custom kitchen with Gaggenau and Sub-Zero
- Elevator clad with high-polish, mirrored nickel

*Offered at $17,995,000*          MLS#: 216003751

Beyond the interior design, this space is centered on 360-degree views. The entire penthouse is outfitted with a range of state-of-the-art LED recessed lighting, beautiful custom furnishings, modern decorative fixtures and versatile LED Kreon art lights to highlight both architectural details and fine art. The flooring is large-format Italian porcelain of 31-by-72-inch slabs that run throughout the interior and exterior of the unit. Crestron and Lutron hybrid automation system for audio, lighting and temperature controls, custom millwork in exotic real wood veneers and high-end Italian melamine are all of note. Custom kitchen has Gaggenau and Sub-Zero appliances, white quartz countertops and a private elevator clad with high-polish mirrored nickel finish. Oversized dual closets, including a cedar closet, sauna, as well as a fitness room with a view. High-end innovative plumbing fixtures, such as the powder room faucet from ceiling and sculptural bathtub in master bath. This penthouse comes completely furnished. Get ready to be in awe!

**Jane Bond**
c 239.595.9515
o 239.434.2424
jane.bond@sothebysrealty.com
janebond.premiersothebysrealty.com

Broad Avenue Office
390 Broad Avenue South
Naples, FL 34102

Premier | Sotheby's
INTERNATIONAL REALTY

This is a level of luxury to behold. Enter into one of the most exclusive penthouses that Naples has ever seen.

# ABOUT THE AUTHOR

Jane Bond grew up in the inner city of Philadelphia. Growing up as a child, she always dreamed of being a boss, a CEO of her own company. While looking back on becoming a boss in several careers, she found real estate to be the most lucrative and rewarding.

Jane Bond, principal of the Bond Group I Diamond Key Service, works with entrepreneurs, career professionals, and individuals in the high-net-worth community generally. Her clients include celebrities, entertainers, and professional athletes, as well as many Wall Street finance executives. Working with clients who demand extremely high levels of excellence from those around them requires Ms. Bond to bring her A-game at all times.

Armed with a background in finance, entertainment, interior design, international travel, and now luxury real estate, Jane brings a wealth of knowledge and experience to her clients' disposal. One client remarked when asked what Jane brings to the table, "Quite simply, Ms. Bond is the table."

Jane has taken the client service experience to next-level concierge luxury status. Going above and beyond is simply the beginning. Her ability to see angles and opportunities that others typically miss is a key weapon in her armory.

Living in a 24-7 global marketplace, Ms. Bond is able to seamlessly facilitate transactions for clients, whether located on the East Coast, West Coast, or internationally. She always advocates for clients with the utmost integrity, knowledge, and business acumen.

Jane recently created an online course for aspiring, new, and seasoned agents where she coaches them from contrast to clarity.

CPSIA information can be obtained
at www.ICGtesting.com
Printed in the USA
FSHW011710020321